CAMBRIDGE LIBRARY COLLECTION

Books of enduring scholarly value

History

The books reissued in this series include accounts of historical events and movements by eye-witnesses and contemporaries, as well as landmark studies that assembled significant source materials or developed new historiographical methods. The series includes work in social, political and military history on a wide range of periods and regions, giving modern scholars ready access to influential publications of the past.

The Merchants' and Mariners' African Guide

This work of 1822 was written by Royal Navy Lieutenant Edward Bold to help sailors navigate from Britain to West Africa, via Madeira, the Canaries and the Cape Verde Islands. Bold was concerned about 'excessively erroneous hydrographic descriptions' that misled ships and put crews in danger. Writing after Britain's abolition of the slave trade, Bold was an advocate of developing other types of commerce with this region of Africa – an area, as he discovered, rich in valuable ivory – and part of the work describes the system of trade that stretched from port to port along the continent's western coast, including useful information such as that, upon arriving, sailors should indicate their desire to trade by 'firing a gun and hoisting your colours'. With its navigational detail and observations about trade, this work is a useful source on Anglo-African commerce in the nineteenth century.

T0382558

Cambridge University Press has long been a pioneer in the reissuing of out-of-print titles from its own backlist, producing digital reprints of books that are still sought after by scholars and students but could not be reprinted economically using traditional technology. The Cambridge Library Collection extends this activity to a wider range of books which are still of importance to researchers and professionals, either for the source material they contain, or as landmarks in the history of their academic discipline.

Drawing from the world-renowned collections in the Cambridge University Library, and guided by the advice of experts in each subject area, Cambridge University Press is using state-of-the-art scanning machines in its own Printing House to capture the content of each book selected for inclusion. The files are processed to give a consistently clear, crisp image, and the books finished to the high quality standard for which the Press is recognised around the world. The latest print-on-demand technology ensures that the books will remain available indefinitely, and that orders for single or multiple copies can quickly be supplied.

The Cambridge Library Collection will bring back to life books of enduring scholarly value (including out-of-copyright works originally issued by other publishers) across a wide range of disciplines in the humanities and social sciences and in science and technology.

The Merchants'
and Mariners'
African Guide

*The Coast, Bays, Harbours, and Adjacent
Islands of West Africa*

Edward Bold

CAMBRIDGE UNIVERSITY PRESS

Cambridge, New York, Melbourne, Madrid, Cape Town,
Singapore, São Paolo, Delhi, Tokyo, Mexico City

Published in the United States of America by Cambridge University Press, New York

www.cambridge.org
Information on this title: www.cambridge.org/9781108030663

© in this compilation Cambridge University Press 2011

This edition first published 1822
This digitally printed version 2011

ISBN 978-1-108-03066-3 Paperback

THE

MERCHANTS' AND MARINERS'

AFRICAN GUIDE;

CONTAINING

AN ACCURATE DESCRIPTION OF

THE COAST, BAYS, HARBOURS,

AND ADJACENT ISLANDS OF

West Africa,

WITH THEIR CORRECTED LONGITUDINAL POSITIONS;

COMPRISING A STATEMENT OF THE

SEASONS, WINDS, AND CURRENTS,

PECULIAR TO EACH COUNTRY;

TO WHICH IS ADDED,

A MINUTE EXPLANATION OF THE VARIOUS

SYSTEMS OF TRAFFIC,

THAT ARE

ADOPTED ON THE WINDWARD AND GOLD COAST,

As well as the Principal Ports to Leeward;

ALSO,

A FEW HINTS TO THE MERCANTILE NAVIGATOR,

Suggesting a Means of securing more rapid Passages, both to and from the
Coast, than have hitherto been practised;

WITH

THREE CORRECT DRAUGHTS,

From recent Surveys by the Author,

OF THE PORTS OF BENIN, CALLEBAR AND PRINCES.

By LIEUT. EDWARD BOLD, R. N.

London:

PRINTED FOR J. W. NORIE AND CO.

(Successors to the late William Heather.)

CHARTSELLERS TO THE ADMIRALTY AND THE HONORABLE EAST INDIA COMPANY;
AT THE NAVIGATION WAREHOUSE AND NAVAL ACADEMY,

No. 157, Leadenhall Street.

1822.

Price Six Shillings in Boards.

CONTENTS.

-~&~-

INTRODUCTION.

⸺••◉••⸺

THE Western Coast of Africa though explored and frequented by the Portuguese as early as the fourteenth and fifteenth centuries, still remains most erroneously described with regard to its hydrography as well as the interior history, many important parts totally unsurveyed, the latitudes and longitudes of which have only been guessed at and communicated by persons, whose scientific knowledge has been too circumscribed to enable them to ascertain, with accuracy, the position of places.

The great cause of such an extensive tract of country continuing so imperfectly known to us, is the paucity of navigable rivers, added to the extreme unhealthiness of the climate, which is so decidedly inimical to the European constitution, that it precludes every inducement, in many parts, to establish settlements for commercial purposes, that principal source from whence we derive our local acquaintance with foreign countries, and whereby we can alone hope for a place like Africa, emerging from so melancholy a state of ignorance, barbarism, and irreligion.

Commerce may be said to be the *primum mobile* of all foreign adventure, for it is to it alone we are indebted for our knowledge, and the civilization of distant countries, and is the great stimulus to nautic research, consequently, the more a coast is resorted to for commercial purposes, the more it becomes essential for the navigator to exercise and extend his nautic skill.

It necessarily then imposes a duty on every individual, either interested in the cause of humanity, patriotism, or commerce, to collect and communicate any knowledge, however trifling, that may have a tendency to generalize improvement, or facilitate the adventures and operations of the merchant or mariner; for it is only by the aid of time and a gradual progress, that we can possibly cherish the expectations of attaining that perfection which solely depends on experience.

Under these impressions the present work is undertaken, an inducement to which has arisen from the author's own experience of many excessively erroneous hydrographic descriptions, whereby ships are much misled, and frequently greatly endangered: the longitudinal errors, in particular, are palpably glaring all down the coast, from Cape St. Ann as far as the Congo, which in many parts is nearly a degree to the East or West of what is expressed in the generality of tables, or laid down in the various charts.

Africa, notwithstanding the many allurements it holds out for adventure to the commercial world, since the abolition of the slave trade, has been very little resorted to, particularly to the Southward of the Gold Coast, in the Bights of Benin, Biaffra, and at Cameroons, where the trade is principally monopolized by the Liverpool vessels, on account of their facility for procuring fine salt, and at an infinite cheaper rate than at any other port, which article constitutes a very material and essential part of the cargo for those places. The knowledge also of the trade, remains still but very circumscribed, being confined to a trifling number of masters of vessels, whose considerable profits render it unquestionably an object of peculiar interest to them, exclusively to retain, if possible, such lucrative advantages. Hence arise the many serious losses, merchants must necessarily experience by the sickness, or death of the master, in whom all trust is confided, and on whom solely depends the success of the voyage; with him then die all the interests of the adventure and the vessel; for the command of the ship and guidance of affairs, devolving on the succeeding officer who, generally speaking, being in total ignorance of the trade, or the ship's concerns, must inevitably cause the most decided failure of the owner's prospects.

It is presumed then, this work will prove adequate effectually to avert those disastrous occurrences to the merchant, and at the same time enable every young man engaged in this voyage and trade, to make himself perfect master of its hitherto considered mysteries, in a comparatively short period, and fully capacitate him to succeed or represent his captain in the event of sickness, death, or any other emergency, and to acquit himself to the satisfaction of his employers, to whom he looks for patronage and preferment.

No country is more susceptible than the West Coast of Africa, of affording to the commercial world, the most ample resources, if roused from their present lethargy to a state of industry and labour, which can only be accomplished by means of a frequent intercourse with civilized nations, through whom they may acquire ideas of refinement, education, and religion, to stimulate them to those occupations which largely and most effectually contribute to ultimate national opulence and aggrandizement.

To rescue then this extensive Continent from the grasp of slavery, and efficiently to accomplish the total abolition of a practice, so abominable, and degrading to mankind as a social being; to civilize and conduct its rude natives to the path of Christianity, and to generalize and extend the beneficial effects of its commerce, becomes altogether a duty and question of state; the success of its completion, solely and totally depending on the patronage and encouragement of civilized government.

Colonization is the first great operative means of carrying into effect all exertions in such a cause; secondly, the establishment of schools for the tuition of the yet unbigotted *juvenile* branches, according to our present national system of education; by which means civilization and Christianity would become generally disseminated; which progressively increasing with succeeding generations, would insensibly, yet radically obliterate the destructive effects of heathen superstition, and exalt them to a degree of independence, and at the same time to a more dignified rank in the estimation of refined powers. Thirdly, as far as relates to the Commerce of this Country, it may be possitively asserted, an incitement to its more frequent pursuit, can only be *effectually* held out, by a considerable diminution of the duties on all its articles of produce; whereby the government revenue arising from the trade instead of experiencing any decrease, must eventually augment in a fourfold ratio, by means of the rapid addition it would necessarily cause in the number of its adventurers; independent of which, the noble views of Christianity would be forwarded by a considerable and speedy amelioration in the condition of a rude and barbarous race.

By cultivation, also, the country would be divested of a great proportion of its pernicious effects, since it is a well-known fact, the unhealthiness of its climate very principally arises from its present uncultivated state.

The excellence and amenity of its soil, the luxuriance and richness of its indigenous productions, vegetable, as well as mineral, are unequalled in any part of the known world, and only require the hand of labour and industry to make them generally known, and subservient to the uses of mankind.

No means or exertions ought then to be spared in endeavouring to facilitate an access to such promising shores, or to develope the nature of its trade, for the benefit of every individual who is desirous of promoting associations with a part of the globe that still remains in its earliest state of infancy, and must, consequently, prove an annual and inexhaustible source of mutual commercial improvement and advantage to both natives and adventurers. In order to meet such sentiments, a system of traffic is connected with the work which lays open an explanation of the various branches of commerce that exist along the windward coast, and the principal and most frequented places of trade to leeward.

DIRECTIONS FOR SAILING

COAST OF AFRICA.

—◆—

Directions for Sailing to the Madeiras.

IT is too frequently the custom for merchant vessels, bound out of the channel to Madeira or the Canaries, to shape a direct course to the point of destination, particularly when in possession of a leading wind; concluding thereby to ensure a short and favorable passage; but such is the very great uncertainty of the winds in these latitudes, that a few hours may see you labouring under every concurring disadvantage of both wind and weather; and the known prevalence of strong westerly breezes endanger your being embayed in the gulph of Biscay, where, in case of blowing hard, your voyage is not only protracted, probably for weeks, but you have to contend against a lee shore, and at the same time a most excessive heavy and distressing swell, which does the vessel more injury than a voyage to and fro across the Atlantic. It is therefore advisable in sailing out of the English Channel, or rounding Cape Clear out of the Irish Channel, to stretch well to the westward, edging away by degrees to the South, according as the time of year or appearances of the weather suggest, which seamen, generally speaking, are more or less capable of interpreting.

It is necessary to observe, in making passages over this part of the Atlantic, no general currents exist, as many authors have stated and attempted to account for, it being, however, a well ascertained fact, that currents are induced by the operation of uniform winds, allowances must be made, in proportion, to the length of time any certain wind has prevailed, and the force with which it has blown.

These observations, however, are not to preclude the mariner from exercising his judgement in exceptionable cases, which for instance oftentimes occur in cold weather, at the beginning and fall of the year, in the character of N.E. Easterly, or S.E. gales, which at these seasons not unfrequently set in, and prevail for weeks together; consequently, if the weather is observed to be settled, and the wind from these quarters, it would be prudent not to make more Westing than to pass Cape Finisterre at a distance of three or four degrees.

It rarely happens that ships bound to the coast of Africa have any thing to do at Madeira, in which case there is no necessity to make that island, but on ascertaining Porto Santo, shape a course for the Canaries.

PORTO SANTO, lies about 40 miles to the N.E. of Madeira, is excessively remarkable, and may be easily discriminated from the latter place, by its appearing in three large high hummacks, which are discerned in fine weather as far distant as 20 leagues : It has on the S.W. side a roadsted, equal in many respects to Funchal, where there is a neat little town, that produces refreshments and plenty of water.

To the Northward of the island, there is a ledge of rocks about nine miles distant, on a bank extending East and West, terminating in a reef, the shoalest part of which has five fathoms, at the following bearings: the N.E. point of Porto Santo, by compass S.S.E. and the Ilhea da Fonte, or Northermost rock S. by W.

THE DESERTAS, which receive their appellation from the Portuguese on account of their being uninhabited, are two long rocky islands, lying nearly N. and S. by compass; when they bear W. by N. they appear separate, Bujio or the Southermost of which is the smallest; there is a free passage between, which, however, ought not to be attempted, but in cases of great emergency, or dire necessity : But between Madeira and the Desertas, there is a fine open passage, eight miles in breadth, having no danger but what is seen, and a strong current setting through to the S.W. it is therefore advisable for vessels coming from the Eastward, with the wind N.E. to frequent this passage; particularly as the N.E.

winds oftentimes produce eddies from the mountains sufficiently strong to prevent ships approaching from the Eastward, and indeed to blow them off altogether; observe therefore to steer as near midchannel as possible, without too soon borrowing on the Madeira shore, where you are liable to be materially annoyed by the calms and eddies off Brazen Head.

On leaving the Desertas you will soon discover the roadsted of Funchal, steering for whence, Loo Rock and Fort, appear a little to the Westward of the town, which with the Citadel in one, bearing about N.N.E. and Funchal Steeple N.E. ¼ N. will give you good anchorage in 35 fathoms, also Loo Rock at a distance of about half a mile with the Citadel a little open to the Eastward, in from 20 to 30 fathoms. To the West of the roads the ground is foul and rocky, deepening as you advance to the East, with a stiff clay bottom. When blowing fresh from the S.W. the Citadel, well open to the Westward is considered a desirable birth.

The road of Funchal is perfectly exposed from the West to the S.E.; consequently from these points the winds are strongest, and ships on the appearance of a menacing atmosphere to the Southward or S.W. ought to take every precaution and be in readiness to go out of the roads at a moment's warning.

In summer there are regular land and sea breezes, the latter setting in from the S.W. in the forenoon, and off shore towards nine or ten o'clock in the evening, sometimes as late as midnight; the land breezes do not extend more than two or three miles from the shore, but when it blows fresh in the offing the true wind prevails in the road.

The rainy season is in January, February, and March, when it blows sometimes excessively hard, at which season it is frequently dangerous to remain at the anchorage; and during this period of the year, the surfs on the beach are so incredibly violent, as to prevent a possibility of landing any where but behind the Loo Rock.

Sailing out of Funchal you should particularly observe to make sail with the land wind, standing directly out to the offing, on account of calms which prevail, under the West and S.W. parts of the island, which have been known to detain vessels for days.

Directions for Sailing through the Canaries.

Between Madeira and the Canaries there is a cluster of rocks and islands called the Salvages, bearing due North, about 27 leagues from Point Naga in Teneriffe ; they are rather dangerous to pass in the night, but a South course from Funchal will give them a good birth to the Eastward ; they consist of a number of rocks and three small islands ; viz. the great Salvage, the great Piton, and the little Piton, and may be seen as far as 20 miles off in fine weather, they lie N.N.E. and S.S.W. connected with each other by a ledge of rocks ; the Northernmost or Great Salvage being in lat. 30° 9′ N. and the Southernmost or little Piton 30° N. There is anchorage with fine sandy bottom on the S.E. side of the Great Salvage, between which and the Great Piton it is navigable.

Vessels bound to the Coast of Africa from the North, are advised to go between Palma and Teneriffe, having generally speaking found the breeze fresher and more continued through that passage than any other, and the calms of less duration, notwithstanding the intervening land is so considerably higher ; but it is necessary to observe you should keep amid-channel or rather borrow on the Palma shore, to avoid getting too soon under the lee of Teneriffe.

The Channel is about 40 miles in breadth and perfectly free from the least possible danger, having on both sides excessively high land with a bold shore.

PALMA. This island is prodigiously high, and may under any circumstances be descried at a considerable distance, consequently run for with the greatest confidence at any period of the night. It has two ports, Santo Cruz and Tassacorta, the former of which is the most considerable, lying on the East side in 28° 42′ N. and 17° 40′ W. The town and shipping are only to be discerned within a short distance, on account of the land being uncommonly steep close behind; it is therefore suggested to the novice in these parts to edge into the Northward, and run down along shore that he may not get to the Southward of the road which lies within half a mile of the town, where vessels may ride with safety in 12 to 20 fathoms during all winds. Tassacorta is on the S.W. side in 28° 38ʰ N. and 17° 50ʰ W. a place of no note, and being exposed to Westerly winds is only frequented by fishing boats.

FERRO, is the Westernmost of the Canaries ; La Dabessa or the Westernmost point being in 18° 2ʹ W. and 27° 40ʹ N. It does not boast the possession of either town, roads, or production of any consideration, therefore is unworthy the attention of navigators, which renders minute detail here totally unnecessary.

GOMERO, is somewhat larger than Ferro, and lies about 14 miles S.W. from the South of Teneriffe, its principal town is St. Sebastian, in 28° 8ʹ N. and 17° 1ʹ W. being situated at the bottom of a commodious bay on the East side, where vessels may ride in 10 to 15 fathoms, entirely land locked from all but S.E. winds ; it is essential to be securely moored here on account of the strong eddies, particularly off the land, which oftentimes come in severe gusts.

TENERIFFE. Point Naga or the N.E. end of this island lies about 16 leagues W.N.W. from the Isletta, or the N.E. point of Canaria. The celebrated Peak, more familiarly known to the inhabitants by the appellation of Teyde, lies rather over to the Western side of the island, and is generally speaking overcapped with clouds, it is distinctly seen at a distance of 100 miles, and on a beautifully clear day, when receding from it, may be retained perfect to the eye as far as 130 miles. The islanders boast of its being seen 160 miles off, which, however is dubious and almost impossible; for although its height might extend beyond the sensible horizon, the atmospheric medium of the intervening distance would totally envelope it, and preclude the possibility of its being rendered visible. The principal port of this island is Santa Cruz on the East side about 16 miles from Point Naga, in lat. 28° 28ʹ N. long. 16° 22ʹ W. its road is convenient, extending from 6 fathoms, or a cable's length from the shore, to 35 fathoms three-quarters of a mile distant. The inner anchorage is rocky and foul ground, with outside a soft oozy bottom, in 20 or 35 fathoms a little to the Northward of the town, being decidedly the most preferable position for all vessels. The island abounds in every species of fruit and vegetables, with plentiful supplies of fresh water. It is, however,

c

necessary to guard the stranger against the fraudulent and predatory habits of the natives, most particularly those who frequent the vessels with articles of every nature for sale.

OROTAVA, is on the Western side of the island, nearly 28 miles S.W. of Point Naga, its roadsted is perfectly open and exposed, with anchorage only in 40 and 50 fathoms, therefore does not offer a desirable retreat to navigators.

CANARIA. This island is excessively lofty and mountanious towards the middle, terminating on the N.E. by the Isletta, a peninsula, which lies 46 miles, as nearly West as possible, from the Southernmost point of Fuertaventura. The peninsula is in 28° 13′ N. and 15° 25′ W. about eight miles in circumference, connected with the island by a narrow isthmus, two miles and a half in length, each side of which forms an extensive bay; the one to the Eastward is called Puerto de Luz, a spacious sandy bay, with good anchorage in 10 to 30 fathoms, for vessels of all burthens, from within half a mile N.E. of the town, to a mile and a half; the latter of which is preferable on account of there being much better ground: there are several steep rocks at the entrance on the N.E. side, which protect the shipping, and you may lie secure from all winds excepting the S.E. to which the bay is altogether exposed, however instances of its blowing sufficiently fresh from that point to endanger ships, rarely occur here. Palmas, the capital of the island, is a large town situated at the bottom of the bay, to the N.W. of which there is a fine smooth landing place, where plentiful supplies of water and refreshments may be obtained.

The bay on the West side is open to the sea, exposed to heavy swells and N.W. winds, consequently only frequented by fishing boats and vessels of very inferior burthen, that shelter between a ledge of rocks and the shore.

Three or four leagues farther to the S.E. of Puerto de Luz lies the town and port of Ganao, where there is good anchorage, secured from all winds excepting the South, but is very little frequented.

FUERTAVENTURA, lies about 15 miles to the S.W. of Lancerota, at the North end there is a small uninhabited island, called Lobos, between which and the main is very good anchorage with sandy bottom; the best situation s amid channel, with the East point of

Lobos bearing N.E. ½ N. This road though open and apparently exposed, is perfectly safe, with almost invariably smooth water. Close to the shore on the Fuertaventura side, there is a good well, where boats may water with the utmost facility.

The channel between this island and Lancerota, is termed the Bocayna, and vessels sailing through here from the Eastward with the trade wind, will lose the breeze when under the lee of Lancerota, and find baffling winds at S.W. therefore ought to ply to windward on the Lobos side, where they will soon get a steady Northerly breeze to carry them through. It is unnecessary to close too near on Lobos, the ground there being excessively foul and rocky, which creates breakers of an incredible height.

LANCEROTA, is a dark rocky looking island, and may be descried at a considerable distance, it terminates to the North by Graciosa, a small barren island in 29° 19′ N. and 13° 30′ W. the channel between which and the main forms a spacious harbour, called El Rio, commodious for vessels of any burthen, but not very smooth with the N.E. trades. On the S.E. side there are two more ports, Puerto de Naos and Puerto de Cavallos, but their entrances shallow, the former having only 17 feet at high water spring tides, and the latter 12 feet; they are separated and defended by a castle which stands on a small island. About two leagues and a half to the Northward of Graciosa, there is another island called Allegranza, and 4½ leagues N.N.E. of the Northernmost point of Lancerota, or the Punta del Farrion, is a large high rock, called the East Rock, and between the two islands to the Westward a dangerous one, called the West Rock; which ought not to be approached without the greatest caution in the night, on account of the currents that are frequently rapid, and set directly in amongst them; especially on the full and change of the moon.

There remains to be remarked, that in sailing between the whole of the Canaries no danger exists but what is perfectly discernible, excepting a sunken rock, which also is dubious, however it is as well to guard against the possibility of its existence; the bearings being South end of Teneriffe, W.N.W. 21 miles, and Port of Gando, East, 14 miles.

On the Winds and Calms peculiar to the Canaries.

In the vicinity of these islands, brisk trades are, generally speaking, most prevalent from N.E. to N. throughout the year; they, however, are found sometimes to give place to N.W. and S.W. breezes, the latter of which, not unfrequently blow for a continuance of ten days. And on account of the enormous height of the mountains, when near the land, you are subject to strong gusts and eddy winds, blowing in an opposite direction to that outside, which the navigator ought to avail himself of when beating to windward.

Vessels sailing through, most commonly carry the breeze a few leagues to the Southward of the islands, more or less, according to the strength and direction of the wind, which if far North will take you more to the Southward, and the contrary if to the Eastward.

On approaching the calms, you will find a heavy disagreeable bubbling swell, but not so violent as Capt. Glass seems to have described, the sea breaks and is very irregular, consequently produces a distressing motion to the ship, which renders it necessary to take advantage of every breath of wind to get to the Southward.

These calms are occasioned by the intervening high land of the Canaries obstructing the regular course of the trades, and extend from 10 to 30 leagues to leeward, in proportion to the power of the breeze outside; for sailing between Palma and Teneriffe with strong trades I have recovered the breeze at not more than ten leagues distant, and at another time, with light winds, farther than thirty. And it may be observed, when the trades are light, the calms are more extensive, at which time, however, light S.W. breezes prevail; and on the contrary, when they are strong, the calms are very circumscribed, but not the slightest air within sometimes for days.

Between the Canaries and the Cape Verdes a current runs to the S.W. at the rate of half a knot, increasing as you approach the islands, for which reason it is considered decidedly better to keep a little inside the Porgus bank, towards the main, if bound to the Coast of Guinea, there being no necessity to make Cape Verde, particularly as the wind is invariably fresher amid channel.

In about the latitude of 14° and 16° N. the trades begin to lose their strength, veering gradually round from the Northward to the N.W. and from thence to the Westward and S.W. as you draw in with the Coast of Africa, in the latitude of 7° and 10° N.

Coast of Africa from Cape Spartel to Cape Bogador.

The only place, or port between Cape Spartel and Cape Verde that is worth considering, or much frequented by European traders, is Mogador; consequently, as vessels bound to Sierra Leon and Guinea, have no business on this coast, it will be unnecessary to enter into the minutiæ of descriptive detail, any farther than what may serve to guide the mariner in cases of emergency, or any unforeseen cause which may drive him here.

The first and most essential thing to be observed on approaching this coast, is the indraught or current which sets on shore to the Eastward, with a heavy swell close to the shore, that increases the danger of a near approach. The want of attention to this very material consideration, has occasioned innumerable, and recent deplorable instances of shipwreck, particularly near the inhospitable shores of the Desart, where the fostering hand of humanity is never tendered, commiseration is a stranger, and where the wretched castaway is dragged into slavery by the savage Moorish hordes, who frequent that coast to obtain an existence at the expence of their fellow-creatures.

CAPE SPARTEL is in 35° 49′ N. latitude, 5° 57′ W. longitude from which place to the town of Arzilla, the coast lies nearly S. ½ W. 20 miles, and may be recognized by its distant high mountains inland, with 30 fathoms coarse ground, a league and a half off shore.

The land between Arzilla and El Arraiche, is easily distinguished by a remarkable white patch, which is seen nearly fifteen miles off; the town stands on the river El Kos, and is recognizable on a near approach by a large castle and batteries.

THE PEAK OF FAS, is a high mountain inland, of a conic form, and is the mark for the old town of Marmora, in lat. 34, 46 N. 11 leagues S. by W. of which lies new Marmora; all along this coast the swell is sometimes excessive on the shore, which with the S.W. winds render it extremely dangerous.

THE TOWN OF RABAT is situated on the river Bu Regreg, in 34° 7' N. latitude, 6° 40' W. longitude, and is particularly remarkable by a prodigious high tower, called Beni Hassan, which may be discerned 20 miles off with facility in fine weather; there is a bar across the river rendering it only navigable for very small vessels, but there is a good anchorage between the Mosque and the high tower for ships of every burthen, which, however, can only be considered safe from March to the latter end of August. The coast from Rabat to Cape Azamore forms a bight and extends S.W. by W. ½ W. 31 leagues, the latter being in 33° 37' N. lat. 8° 12' W. long. From thence to Cape Blanco, 28 miles in a similar direction, with a very rocky coast, particularly off the town of Mazagou, where a reef extends three or four miles, N. by W. of the town; the mark for the outer limits of which is the centre of the town due South 4 miles, with the high tower of Tid S.S.W. ½ W. From Cape Blanco to Cape Cantin the course is S.W. by S. 13 leagues, where there is a strong current to the S.W. From Cape Cantin to Cape Geer the coast lies about S. by W. ½ W. 42 leagues, 17 miles from the former is the Bay of Saffia, at the bottom of which there is an old town of the same name, good anchorage may be found here in the summer season, from 20 to 30 fathoms, in the centre of the bay.

The only town and port of consequence on this coast, which may be said to retain a regulated intercourse with the European mercantile world, is Mogador, where there is an English consul, it is built on a flat near the sea, surrounded by almost two leagues of sandy desart, without any supplies of fresh water nearer than a mile and a half.

The small island of Suerra to the S.W. of the town, forms the anchorage between it and the main, but only for vessels not drawing more than 10 feet, those of greater draught lying in the bay, two miles to the Westward of the large battery, where however it is exposed, and dangerous in the winter from November to the beginning of February. From hence to Cape Geer the course is S.W. by W. to avoid a rock off Cape Tefelnch. The land about Cape Geer is very remarkable, by a high round hummock in the interior, visible at a distance of 12 miles. On the North side of the Cape there is a ledge of rocks, extending seaward, which you should not approach nearer than 15 fathoms, and 8 leagues W. by N. from the Cape lies Cleaveland's shoal, with only 3 or 4 feet water on it, rendering it advisable to give it a good birth on passing. Five leagues S.E. of the Cape is the town of Santa Cruz, at the bottom of an extensive bay, where there is an excellent well-sheltered anchorage for vessels of all burthens; but the commercial character of this place having totally ceased, it is in consequence no longer frequented.

From Cape Geer to Cape Bogador the course is S.W. ½ S. 120 leagues; the current sets very strong on all this coast, and it is here, particularly, that ships are but too often wrecked and endangered, by getting driven near the shore before they are aware, for the want of calculating the set of the current, so very essential on this coast.

A Description of the Coast from Cape Bogador to Cape Verde.

From Cape Bogador to Cape Blanco the course is about S.S.W. ½ W. 125 leagues, as far as Augra dos Ruivos the land is excessively high and rugged, remarkable for its Peak called Penha Grande; there is good anchorage in Angra Bay to the Northward with fine sandy bottom; 8 leagues to the Southward of the Bay the land is very remarkable by its seven high hills called the Seven Capes; from thence to the entrance of Rio d'Auro it is 18 leagues, where there is very good fishing, but the river is shallow and dangerous, and the only fresh water on this Coast is to be found here; as far as Cape Blanco the Coast is all very foul with a constant hollow roaring surf that is heard at a great distance from the shore, but there is no danger, and the Cape may be rounded pretty close; its appearance is very remarkable, and makes it easily known by its two hills which terminate in very low land to the pitch of the Cape; the Easternmost hill coming from the Northward has a large clump of bushes near the summit.   The Cape is in 20° 55′ N. lat. and 17° 10′ W. long.

CAPE BLANCO TO CAPE VERDE.   The course is S. ¼ W. 120 leagues.   Thirteen miles S. by W. from the former is the formidable bank of Arguin extending as far South as Cape Merrick, where it is met by another small bank, and between which there is a passage nearly 5 miles wide, with 4 fathoms leading into the bay and to the river St. John ; the bank is dangerous and ought carefully to be avoided by vessels making Cape Blanco bound to the Southward; on its North end there is a ledge of rocks forming the entrance of the bay between it and the Cape; and on the West side only 3 fathoms, in many parts with 20 and more close outside ; therefore in coasting down do not approach nearer than 35 fathoms as far as Cape Merrick, and from thence in 10 and 12 fathoms which will take you to the roads of Senegal.   The whole of this coast is low with a sandy shore, except two moderate sized sand hills, between which there is a remarkable bush serving as a mark for the bay of Portendick.

SENEGAL.   This great river is the third in point of magnitude on the West coast of Africa, taking its source on the West side of the Tong mountains, from whence it runs in a N.W. direction with numerous windings upwards of 300 leagues to its mouth, where on a small island the French have a fort and settlement called St. Louis ; it was however first established by the Dutch in 1680, but has since successively passed through the hands of the French and British, until ceded to the latter by the treaty of 1783, and again to the French in 1815, who now hold it.   Being all a low swampy country in the vicinity of the coast, it is excessively unhealthy, particularly between the months of June and November.   The principal and most important article of commerce is gum, which is collected in the greatest abundance by the natives ; elephants' teeth, hides, and bees-wax are also obtained.

On account of the extreme lowness of the land, it is generally found difficult to discover this river, particularly as it is shut in at the mouth, by its taking a Northerly direction from thence ; it is consequently deemed advisable for strangers, and indeed all vessels to make the land to the Northward, where a grove of Palmetto trees 35 miles from the river may serve as an index to their approach. There are frequently down this coast violent ripplings, appearing like breakers, but ought to create no alarm as they are caused by the currents underneath setting on the bank. * Barbary Point which forms the North side of the entrance of this river is in 15° 53′ N. lat. and 16° 34′ W. long. from whence to Mouitte Point and bay, there is a hard sandy and dangerous bar, obstructing the passage for vessels above 9 or 10 feet draught. The anchorage for large vessels is outside in 9 to 12 fathoms, Barbary Point and a large bare tree on the opposite side bearing E. by S. and the Nothernmost land in sight N. by E. ¼ E.; it is very good holding ground, but most commonly a great sea and swell which render it essential to come to, with good ground tackle. The greatest possible care and attention ought to be observed in navigating the bar, which has proved disastrous to so many vessels, on account of the tide operating with such peculiar and incredible force in its vicinity ; when you have opened the river, steer N.E. directly over the bar where you will soon find 7 and 8 fathoms, then keep over to the larboard shore to avoid a bank on the opposite side, and you will have a free passage up to Fort Louis. The number of windings and islands about here create an excessive velocity of tide, which carries down with it those immense quantities of sand that form the bar at the mouth of the river, where it is 1¾ miles in width, with only a navigable passage of 200 fathoms on the South side. The entrance ought not to be attempted, if the weather is bad and the sea setting in, for the impetuosity of the waves which follow in such constant succession

---

* For the benefit of those who are engaged in the commerce of this country, Barbary Point may be suggested as an eligible position to erect a land-mark which is so much wanted to enable the mariner to recognize the port ; and an elevated mast with a cask on the summit painted white, would answer every purpose without creating expense.

create an undulating motion sufficiently violent to overturn a moderate sized vessel ; it is easiest of access from June to October ; at the anchorage outside, the current sets to the S.W. when at the full and change days it is high water at 10^H 30$'$. It may be recommended not to water here if it can be avoided, as all the water is brackish and unhealthy.

From the great bank of Arguin there is a bank of soundings extending 25 miles from the land as far as the Bay of Yoff, with from 60 to 80 fathoms on the outer edge with plenty of good fish.

The Bay of Yoff is particularly dangerous to come near, on account of the current setting directly in, where close to the shore the water is too deep to admit of anchorage ; therefore vessels sailing South ought to keep well to the Westward for rounding the Cape.

CAPE VERDE, lies in 14° 48$'$ N. lat. and 17° 36$'$ W. long. with 16° 30$'$ Westerly variation ; it is very recognizable by its two round hills a few miles inland to the West of the Cape, which have received the appellation of the Paps, the Easternmost is thickly studded with trees, and they terminate by a low land that stretches out to the pitch of the Cape, called Almadia Point, off which there is a reef of rocks extending a league to the Westward. The Paps are discernable in fine weather at a distance of 25 miles, and it is unnecessary to warn the navigator not to mistake for them two small hills of a similar form, which lie 12 leagues to the Eastward ; the direction of the land being considered sufficient to enable them to discriminate.

Cape Verde or Salt Islands.

These islands are ten in number, Bonavista or the Easternmost lies 100 leagues on a parallel to the Westward of Cape Verde ; they were first discovered by the Portuguese from whom they received the following names: Ilha de Sal, Bonavista, Mayo, St. Jago, Iiha de Fogo, Brava, St. Nicholas, Santa Lucia, St. Vincent, and San Antonio. They are of submarine volcanic formation, and boast a climate and vegetation approaching nearer that of the temperate regions.

BONAVISTA. This island (as its appellation expresses) presents a beautiful variegated appearance interspersed with scattered mountains terminating in low points to the water, its North Point is in lat. 16° 5′ N. and 22° 48′ W. long. bearing S. ½ E. 9 leagues from Ilha de Sal, it is the most dangerous of all the islands, on account of its being surrounded by rocks and shoals, also the current setting directly on it from the N.E. The North Point is very low 10 miles East from which, there is a ledge of rocks called the N.E. reef, extending six miles into the sea from Mount Ochel; and another two miles and a half from Brazen Head called the East reef. Between the former there are three passages to the Northward directed by three small visible rocks or keys, the best of which is between a ledge of rocks and the South Key. A vessel may moor in safety three quarters of a mile S.E. of the middle Key, Mount Ochel bearing West in 7 fathoms. The Eastern extremity of the N.E. reef bears due North from Brazen Head, from which the current sets strong to the S.E.

On the N.W. side 5 miles from North Point is English road, formed by a small island half a mile S.W. by S. from which, there is a reef with only 1½ fathom on it; sailing into the road, keep between it and the island edging rather on the latter in about 7 fathoms; the reef extends N.N.E. and S.S.W. but the sea seldom breaks; The best anchorage is Small Island, N. by W. and Man Mountain S. by E. in 6 or 7 fathoms, there is little rise of water, and the tide flows at 2 hours and 30 minutes, full and change days.

Portuguese road is on the S.W. side of the island, where there is anchorage in 6 to 8 fathoms, the Man Mountain N. by W. and S.E. point of the bay S.E. ½ S.; 5 leagues to the West of this road there is a reef on which the water always breaks, therefore easily avoided, and 9 miles South of this reef is Leton's Rock, which is bold with a coral bottom extending several miles to the S.W.; it is a little above water with occasionally excessively high breakers, but in fine weather scarcely any. The profusion of fish in its vicinity is incredible.

BONETTA ROCKS, consist of a reef of rocks, nearly 4 miles in length and 1½ broad, and in consequence of the currents about the

islands are extremely dangerous, which renders it prudent for vessels bound thence to make Ilha de Sal, and accordingly shape a
course to their destination; they lie 31 leagues E. by N. from the
North end of Bonavista. There is said to be another reef 10
leagues E.N.E. from the same point, but of doubtful existence.

ILHA DE SAL, receives its appellation from the quantity of salt
with which it abounds, and is the chief production of the island,
being otherwise particularly noted for its sterility, scarcely presenting to the eye an appearance of verdure, it is long and narrow
stretching from the N.W. to S.E. Coming from the South the land
is very irregular, appearing in some parts very high with intermediate low spaces and sandy hillocks; there are two bays where vessels may ride, and are esteemed better than the generality of road-
steds about these islands, being less subject to those squalls and
indrafts that characterize the bays and harbours of the Cape Verdes;
they lie on the West side North and South of Bird Island, which
latter lies half a mile from the middle Mount; the one to the North
is called Palmera Bay, with from 5 to 8 fathoms, at 1 mile off; and
the one to the South which is the most preferable, is Mordeira
Bay, where there is anchorage in 6 or 7 fathoms; Bird Island
N.W. by N. 2 miles; the ground here as at all the other islands is
rocky. The South Point lies in 16° 38′ N. lat. and 23° 2′ W.
long. where there is a small reef extending 1 mile from the shore
and terminates in a sandy spit.

MAYO is a small island 9 miles in length, distinguished by its
two high mountains on the East side, it is formed of volcanic sub-
stance, combining a considerable proportion of basalt and pumice
stone, and partaking of the same barren nature as the last described;
it is but thinly inhabited as its products afford but a bare subsistence
for the degraded species of human nature that seems to frequent its
inhospitable shores. The whole of the North side is rocky, with
a reef stretching 2 or 3 miles to the Northward, and ought to be
particularly guarded against by vessels to and from Porto Praya;
English road, which is on the S.W. side is the only anchorage here,
having 7 and 8 fathoms, West Point N.N.W. and South Point S.E.
from whence the land appears with three conic hills to the N.E.
Fresh water is extremely scarce here and by no means good.

St. Jago is the most considerable of the Cape Verdes, and being the seat of government is better inhabited and more frequented than the other islands; it lies N.N.W. and S.S.E. about 12 miles in length, and surrounded by steep and perpendicular cliffs, from which the land rises towards the mountains, which appear high and rugged, and most commonly enveloped in mist until 10 or 11 o'clock in the forenoon; the whole of the coast is interspersed with sunken rocks about a mile and a half from the shore, particularly on the West side, where there are also several small islands; the land from the East appears highest towards the middle, terminating very low to the Southward, called the S.E. point; from hence to the East point of Porto Praya, the course is S.W. 2½ leagues; about a league from the former there is a small bay called St. Francis, where there is a grove of date trees and a house, and has been suggested, may, by strangers, be mistaken for Porto Praya, but as it is comparatively so small, and the distance from the point so short, (which are considered sufficient for discrimination) it will be superfluous to particularize any additional warning.

Porto Praya, the principal harbour of this island, is extremely commodious for shipping of every tonnage, extending E. by N. and W. by S. from Point Tubaron to the East Point, two miles and a quarter; off the former there is a dangerous reef running out to the S.W. and ought to be rounded at a respectable distance, for the current sets directly on it, and at periods runs with great rapidity; the breakers on the reef may be seen at some distance. On the West side, within the bay, there is a long rugged island, called the Isle of Quails, between which and the main there is no passage but for boats, it being excessively foul and shallow; from the North end of the island towards the fort there are only from 2 to 3 fathoms, outside of which, to the mouth of the bay, there is good anchorage in 5 to 18 fathoms, the most frequented being rather in the centre, at the following bearings : the West point S.W. and the flag-staff at the town fort N.W. ½ N. in 8 and 10 fathoms, where vessels may lie well sheltered; but there is still a more preferable birth near the East point, particularly for vessels that intend making a short stay, the marks are the East point E. by S. the flag-staff

N.W. by W. and Point Tubaron, W.S.W. in 7 or 8 fathoms, in which position the ground is good, and you are also conveniently situated for fetching out of the bay and weathering the reef, in case of the winds being light or far to the Eastward ; for, excepting during the rains, they are generally from the N.E. and East. Coming to, about here with a fresh breeze, take care to give sufficient scope of cable, it not being particularly good holding ground.

Sailing from the North to Porto Praya the S.E. point makes very low, round which, at a distance of two miles S.W. is Port St. Francis, known by its brown sandy beach, with a grove of date trees, and a house with a long table land above ; from hence you may keep along shore in 10 fathoms as far as Porto Praya, whose bay is first discovered by a species of decayed earthen fortification on its West point, off which the breakers are discerned at a considerable distance ; haul close round the East point which is bold and safe, and may be rounded within a cable's length, in 7 fathoms; you will then open the brown sandy beach, on which you will first discover a large house, soon after a grove of date trees, and then the fort of the town. The town consists of three rows of miserable looking houses, or hovels, constructed of mud and stone, defended by an antiquated fort of 16 guns, within a decayed parapet; it is inhabited by people of every shade and cast, from the European to the Guinea Negro, whose combined indolence and uncleanliness is almost unparalleled in any part of the globe. The bay abounds in many species of fine fish, which constitutes the principal alimentary resources of the poor. The winter months are during the rains, which commence towards the middle of August, continuing, with intermissions, until November and December, at which period the strong Southerly winds prevail, with a set into the bay ; but the remainder of the year the current runs rapidly to the South, with fine breezes between the North and East.

It is recommended to be careful in carrying sail, on account of the sudden gusts and squalls that frequently rush down between the mountains with excessive force, and have recently caused many fatal accidents to vessels, as well as boats, therefore, is deemed prudent for ships approaching the harbour to shorten sail, or be in active preparation for any event of the kind. The town of Porto Praya lies in 14° 55′ N. latitude, and 23° 32′ W. longitude, with 15° 30′ Westerly variation ; the tide flowing on the full and change days at six, with very little rise. There is another bay on the N.E. side, 6 leagues from Bighude Point, called St. Jago, with a town of the same name, which is the capital of the island, but is no longer frequented by vessels, its road being bad and inconvenient ; however water, provisions and refreshments may be had here in greater abundance, and infinitely more moderate, than at any other part of the island ; 10 miles farther North is Porto Formoso, a fine commodious bay, with good anchorage in 7 or 8 fathoms, but little resorted to, excepting by small traders from the islands.

FUEGO. This island lies 12 leagues to the Westward of the latter, appearing like one immense mountain rising out of the sea, to a peak 7,000 feet high ; it is the only supermarine volcano still smoking, and whose eruptions occasionally create sufficient alarm to oblige its inhabitants to retreat for security to the neighbouring islands. About 1½ league off the North end there is a dangerous sunken rock ; and the whole of the Eastern coast is foul to 1½ mile from the shore, but the West side is clear, with anchorage near the town. In fine weather the Peak of Fogo may be seen as far off as 60 or 65 miles.

BRAVA is about 12 miles long, 7 leagues to the Westward of Fuego, with several small islands and sunken rocks on its North end. It has three bays, or roads, where there is good anchorage, two on the N.E. side and one on the West, it produces good water, and an abundant supply of live stock.

ST. NICHOLAS. This island rises in high pyramidal mountains from the sea, it lies N.W. and S.E. about 10 leagues in length, the Eastern extremity of which (or the East Rock, which appears like a sail) bearing W. by S. 22 leagues from Ilha de Sal ; it possesses four or five good roads, three on the South side and two on the West, the most preferable of which is Preguica Bay, which is celebrated for its profuse supplies of fresh water : to anchor here, run into the North side of the bay, within two miles of the shore, where you will have 7 fathoms and good landing for boats close to the water pond. St. George's Bay is the Westernmost of those on the South, known by its high conic mountain, to the left of which there is another mount, with a flag staff on the summit; come to on the North side in 6 or 7 fathoms close to the shore, to avoid a rocky ledge that stretches from the East point, the conic hill bearing E.N.E. and the flag-staff N.N.W.

St. Lucia, lies four leagues N.W. from the nearest point of St. Nicholas, between which to the South there are two uninhabited islands, called Chaon and Round Island; there are two good bays, one on the N.W. side and another on the S.E. the current is generally rapid between these islands, varying from the N.E. to the S.W.

St. Vincent, is nearly three leagues in the same direction from St. Lucia, the channel between which is rendered excessively dangerous by a number of sunken rocks and small islands. On its West side there is a port and bay, called Porto Grande, esteemed the largest and most commodious amongst the Cape Verdes, being sheltered from every wind, and having a bold shore with good anchorage from 6 to 20 fathoms.

St. Antonio. Between this island and the above-mentioned, the passage is free and safe; distant across the nearest part six miles, its land is remarkably high, particularly towards the N.W. where there are two high mountains, the highest of which is called the Sugar Loaf, and is generally overcapped with clouds; it has one principal town and bay to the Eastward, named Santa Cruz, but where the anchorage is bad with a spit on the side.

General Observations.

The winds in the vicinity of these islands, are, generally speaking, from the North to the East, becoming light and variable as the sun approaches their zenith, accompanied with thick hazy weather some distance from the land, but near which, in the bays and harbours (excepting during the rainy season) there are sea and land breezes; the former blowing from 11 or 12 o'clock in the forenoon until 4 or 5 in the afternoon, when the land wind succeeds.

The rains commence about the middle of August, and continue with intermission until November, during which period the winds are strong from the Southward and S.W. with frequent heavy squalls; and it is during these months the inhabitants are so op-pressed with sickness and fatal diseases. Throughout the year there is a constant atmospheric humidity, from which is deposited an abundant proportion of vapour, which circumstance accounts for the temperature of the climate and the extreme luxuriancy of vege-tation in these islands.

The currents in the neighbourhood are for the most part strong to the S.E. therefore vessels bound from the North ought to make al-lowances accordingly, making the island of Sal first, from whence they may with facility and greater security direct their course to any of the others; I should nevertheless advise frequent trials to be made for the current, having found it myself to run occasionally to the N.E. in which case serious errors may originate in the reckoning; the force of the current is generally speaking $\frac{3}{4}$ of a knot.

There is a certain proportion of the sea from 3 or 4 degrees South of these islands as far as the equator, and 6 degrees to the Eastward which seems to be condemned to perpetual calms and heavy rains, and may be accounted for in the following manner:

The sun in his course from East to West occasions a powerful rarefaction of that proportion of the atmosphere immediately in his vicinity, causing a constant stream of wind which rushes after him from the East to supply and equalize the rarefied medium; this wind crossing the continent of Africa loses its power in traversing such an extensive heated body of land, and separates into two veins, which are termed the N.E. and S.E trades; in consequence of which the intermediate space which is specified above, as far as the conflux of the two winds is in a constant state of inaction, receiv-ing from every side the proximated passing clouds, which settle and deposit their waters with sometimes the most unabated fury. The motion of the two powerful elements wind and water are found to operate in an exactly similar manner, therefore at the meeting of these winds as that of tides, there is an irregular motion caused, creating eddies, &c. which give rise to those sudden varied gusts

E

and rains that vessels experience in traversing the equator from the
N.E. to the S.E. trades, and vice versa.*

Between Cape Verde and the above islands there is an immense
bank of soundings in the longitude of 19° and 20° extending as far
as 18° North latitude, called the Porgas Bank, upon which is a
constant undulatory motion and rippling, causing a noise similar to
that of breakers, arising from the action of the waters on the bank
underneath. There is generally good fishing about here.

A Description of the Coast from Cape Verde to Cape Roxo.

Four leagues and a half S.E. ½ S. from the breakers off Almadia
Point is Cape Mansel, between which there are three islands called
the Magdalens, the largest being perforated at its South end, with
a passage sufficiently wide for boats to pass through. One league
E. by N. from the Cape is the island of Goree, which is nothing
more than a rock three-quarters of a mile in length, where the
French have established a strong fort and garrison for the defence of
their trade on that part of the coast ; there is good anchorage on its
East side in 11 fathoms sand and coral, coming whence, take care
to avoid a ledge that lies a quarter of a mile to the S.E.

From Cape Mansel it is 4 leagues E. by S. ¼ S. to the Red Cape,
forming the bay of Rufisk, on whose East side is a large trading

---

* The sea within the vicinity of these islands is particularly remarkable for the immense floating beds of wrack or sea-weed dispersed over its surface, and has given
rise to various opinions as to its place of growth, and whence it is ultimately deposited. It however proves decidedly to be an American plant a species of the Algœ
called the fucus natans, produced from the rocks and shores contiguous to the Florida
Gulph, from whence it becomes detached on arriving at a state of maturity, and carried off by that well known stream to the African Coast, returning from thence again
to the Westward in the course of the trades. It has been a subject of surprise to
many naturalists that this plant should never be found in its withering state, but like
every other species of the vegetable world, it proceeds with equal regularity through
the process, growth, maturity and decay; it certainly continues vegetating for a
considerable period in its detached state, and is supported by the air globules which
cause its buoyancy, but immediately the symptoms of decay manifest themselves the
buoyant principle is lost by the sudden discharge of the globules, and the plant sinks
which accounts for its not being frequently seen in its last stage.

town of the same name; the coast all round the bay is safe and clean to within half a mile from the shore, at which distance are many little dangerous rocks. Three miles from the Red Cape is Cape Naze, from whence to Gambooroo Point it is 10 miles in a similar direction; but as you advance towards the latter, haul off shore, as the water shoals to 2 and 3 fathoms, nearly a league out with rocks inside, as far as the town and factory of Portudal, which is 3 miles S.E. from the Point; hence to Cape Serene it is 13 miles S.E. by S. parallel with which is the Ambooroo Bank 8 miles out, having on it only 1½, 2, and 3 fathoms with very hard sand; between it and the land there is a channel with 5 or 6 fathoms, keeping 4 miles from the shore, until you bring the Cape to bear N.E. by N. then haul out to the Westward a little to avoid the Joal Bank, which lies about 2 leagues from the Point of the same name; the best guide however is to keep in 7 fathoms round the bank, until Palmarin Point bears East. The two last-mentioned Points form the entrance of the river Joal, which is only navigable for very small vessels, having at its mouth but 3 fathoms; from the tail of Joal to the entrance of Salum river* it is 13 miles, with a bank from thence called the Red Bank, stretching out 5 miles from the shore as far as the Bird Islands. The Bird Islands with Cape St. Mary form the entrance of the river Gambia, lying from each other N. by E. and S. by W. distant 4 leagues.

From Cape Verde to the entrance of the Gambia the true course is S.E. ½ S. distance 30 leagues, which may be run with safety in the night by not coming nearer than 9 or 10 fathoms, so as to avoid the Ambooroo and Joal banks. The Bird Islands lie on the Southern extremity of the Red Bank, off the island of Sangalli; the water is shoal round the islands, with 3 fathoms outside the bank, as far as the Broken Islands, which are merely four small elevations from the bank at the mouth of the river Fallanda, 4 miles from the shore. Cape St. Mary is in 13° 6′ N. lat. 16° 40′ W. long. coming from the North it appears with a tract of rising land to the West-

---

* The entrance of the river Salum is the one on the North of the Red Bank, and not on the South near the Bird Islands as mentioned in other sailing directions.

ward gradually declining towards the East as far as Banyan Point which is 3 leagues. The Cape may be recognized with facility, by two considerably high trees and a tuft to the Eastward.

Between the Cape and Banyan Point there are extensive banks called St. Mary's Shoals, running out 6 miles from the land; they are just awash and only break when the breeze is fresh; the North side forms a sort of spit in the direction of the Broken Islands, between which the distance is scarcely 5 miles.

Three leagues S. by E. from these islands is Barra Point, which with Banyan Point forms the narrows, and has a passage only 3 miles and a half across with a prodigious rapidity of tide, particularly at the ebb (being the most powerful) and nearly runs 9 hours.

Off Barra Point there are some rocks about a mile out, from whence to Dogs' Island on the same shore the distance is 9 miles, and fourteen from Dogs' Island to James Island, and Old Fort.

Sailing into the river Gambia keep over towards the Bird Islands in 5 or 6 fathoms, as far as the Broken Islands (coming no nearer St. Mary's Shoals than 6 fathoms) and when Banyan Point bears South, steer for Barra Point as you will then be clear of the banks, but avoid approaching nearer than 6 fathoms, there being on both sides 5 fathoms, and the next cast but 3. The flood sets directly on Barra Point, and the ebb over the shoals, which in the event of light winds renders it necessary to have an anchor in readiness to obviate any danger; when abreast of Barra Point, distant 1 mile, keep amid channel until you bring Dogs' Island to bear North, on account of a small reef which lies to the Southward of it, also an extensive shoal from the island as far as Barra Point, with only from 1 to 3 fathoms on it. From Dogs' Island to James Island the channel is clear on both sides within a mile of the shore, (excepting off Lemaine Point, which keep full 1 mile and a half from, until well round) and good anchorage, with soft bottom all the way up. If beating up or down do not come nearer than 6 fathoms on either shore as far as Dogs' Island, and 5 from thence to James Island. There is good anchorage in 4 fathoms at the French factory of Albreda, 1 mile and a half from the shore; also between the island and the British factory in 5 fathoms. A short distance up the

Gambia, the English (under the direction of the Governor of Sierra Leon) have established the new settlement called St. Mary's, which promises flattering prospects and acquisitions to the mercantile world, since it has already become a considerable point of attraction to the natives of the contiguous countries, who are concentrating their traffic within its vicinity. The only drawback to its interests is much to be feared will arise from the extreme unhealthiness of the river.

There are also a considerable number of abandoned .French and English establishments all the way up this river, which is navigable for vessels of burthen 70 leagues up, as far as the Port of Cassan. The variation at the entrance of the Gambia is 15° 40′ West, the tide flowing at the full and change at 10ᴴ 30′ with a rise of 7 or 8 feet. The winds on this part of the coast are generally from the N.W. excepting during the winter months of December, January, February and March, when they are between the N.E. and E.S.E. and is considered the most healthy season of the year.

Cape St. Mary to Cape Roxo.

Fourteen miles S.W. by W. from the pitch of the Cape, are the Tongui Rocks and shoal, which run out 4 miles from the Point, or Bald Cape; and from thence to Cape Roxo it is 18 leagues, which you may run with safety in the dark, keeping in 6 or 7 fathoms, to avoid the bank that extends one league from the shore; there are four rivers before you come to the Cape; Casamanza, or the Southernmost of which, is the only one accessible, having 3 fathoms at the entrance, with rocks on each side. The land about the Cape is low, with a sandy beach, near which are some remarkable trees.

From Cape Roxo to Sierra Leon, including the Rio Grande,
its Shoals, and the Isles de Loss.

From Cape Roxo to the East point on the North side of the mouth Chacheo River, the coast lies about 9 leagues E. by S. the navigation of which is rendered excessively difficult by the numerous banks that are interspersed in its vicinity.   Falulo Bank, is 5 leagues in length and 3 miles from the shore, on the same parallel; its West point bearing S.E. from the Cape.   Chacheo Bank, which runs out as far as Jatt's Island ; and between the two, on the West side, a small bank with rocks, called the Middle Bank.   There are passages between them all, the least of which is between the Middle Bank and Falulo, and is as follows : When abreast of the Cape, stand to the S.E. by S. until you bring it to bear N.N.W. 2 leagues, having at the same time 5 or 6 fathoms, then steer E. by S. a little southerly, keeping in 4 fathoms until Falulo Cape bears N.W. 5 or 6 miles, when you will shoal your water, and must keep away S.E. to avoid the North bank and rocks, until the river is perfectly open, and the East point bears N.E. you may then stand directly in for the river, giving a good birth to the Mata Bank, which runs out 5 miles from the town, and is dry on its outer edge, with 3 fathoms abreast ; from hence you may run up as far as the fort, in 5, 6 and 7 fathoms, where there is good anchorage, and many Portuguese settlements in the vicinity.

Sailing out, past the Isle of Cayo, steer S.W. from the East point, until it bears N.E. 5 or 6 miles, in 4 fathoms; then S.E. towards Jatt's Island, until you open the river of that name, and the Island of Cayo bears South, when you may run for the island, keeping it open on the larboard bow; there are two more islands to the Eastward of Cayo, but inaccessible, on account of their approach being obstructed by a mud bank, excepting on the West side of Cayo, which is bold.

Vessels coming direct for the Rio Grande, of course take the Bissagos channel, which is formed by the Chacheo Bank and a spit of hard sand, 12 leagues S. by W. ½ W. from the Cape, over which the tide sets strong at the ebb. On making Cape Roxo steer South 7 leagues, which will bring you into 7 or 8 fathoms, from whence you will nearly find the same sounding, with an E.S.E. course as far as the Island of Cayo, 13 leagues. The island is high and very easy to be discovered at a considerable distance ; if beating come no nearer than 6 fathoms, between Chacheo banks and the South Shoals, where there are heavy breakers off Warang Island.

From Cayo, the same course 25 leagues will take you to St. Martin's, or the West point at the Southern extremity of Bissao's Island, leaving Parrot Island on the right, the former is distinguishable by a remarkably large tree, abreast of which there is a small ledge, also 3 leagues to the South of it a shoal and breakers.

There are extensive Portuguese settlements on Bissao's Island, the principal of which is opposite Sorcerer's Island, lying 5 leagues E.N.E. from the West point, with a clear channel one mile from the shore, and a commodious roadsted abreast the convent between the island and the Portuguese village, where considerable sized vessels are built. The tide flows there at 12 on full and change days.

When a little to the Eastward of St. Martin's point, with Hens' Island and Boolam ditto, well open, steer S.S.E. direct through, taking care to avoid the shoals on each side South of the islands, but as soon as you are in 20 fathoms, and the South point of Mantere Island bears S.E. one league, steer N.E. amid channel until you are in 30 fathoms, with Tombaly point S.E. (which is the South side of Rio Grande) from thence you may run up the river past Bissago Island without danger, which is navigable 150 leagues from the mouth ; the velocity of the tide in this river is excessively great, it is high water on full and change days at 12, with nine feet rise. The flood sets in strong, between the shoals from the S. and S.E. and returns with the ebb in the opposite direction ; North of the shoals the flood sets in from the N.W. and the current without all, to the S.E. at the rate of 12 miles in the twenty-four hours. These shoals are decidedly known to change their position at different periods of the year, therefore require much caution to approach. The shoals of Rio Grande are bounded on the West by the spit of sand before-mentioned, and Poulas Island lying from each other N.W. and S.E. 45 leagues; the former being in latitude 11° 43′ N. longitude 16° 45′ W. the latter in 10° 10′ N. and 15° 5′ W. to clear which and the shoals of St. Ann, steer S.W. by S. (by compass) 15 leagues and S.S.E. 120, coming no nearer either than 20 fathoms, which will bring you into the latitude of Cape Mount, when you may haul in to the Eastward.

To the Southward of the shoal, there is a passage for vessels bound out of the Gambia to the Westward, steering to the W.S.W. along Boslam Islands, past the Hogs' Islands, round the South of Canabac, and to the Westward between it and Mare Island, keeping rather towards the North side of the Channel, on account of the many reefs and shoals that lie between Mantere and Mare Islands, some of which are visible and break at half tide. South of the latter, one league, lies Honey Island, and between it and Paulas an extensive shoal, dry in parts at the low water with only a very narrow passage close to the South side of Honey Island; 13 leagues E. by S. from Paulas there is another small dangerous islet, called Alcatras, surrounded by banks, and a reef extending to the N.N.W. about 5 miles.

Sailing out of the river to the Southward, run down as far as Cove Island, in 6 or 7 fathoms, about two leagues from the land to clear the bank, taking care to avoid the Bache, which is rocky and shoal to 2 fathoms; the N.E. edge of it is 5 leagues West of Cove Island, and 4 from its nearest opposite shore.

From Tombaly Point to Cove Point, (which is the N.W. side of the Noone's entrance) it is 20 leagues; when the latter bears about N.W. and South Point on its opposite bank bears East you will be in 7 or 8 fathoms, in a fair way for the river. Due South of the last-mentioned point, there are breakers and a shoal, six miles in length, some parts dry at low water.

Sailing in, keep over within a mile and a half of South Point; for the river is interspersed with banks to nearly 5 miles from the opposite side, from hence to North Point (the entrance of Talagos river) it is 2 leagues with a channel of 4, 5, and 6 fathoms, but between which there is a shoal to be avoided, by not bringing the North point to bear farther North than E.N.E.; the Channel there is only 1 mile and a half broad, but good anchorage round the Point in 5 fathoms abreast the river.

At the mouth of the Noones it is high water on the full and change days, at 11ᴴ with a rise of 9 feet; the river is navigable 10 leagues up for vessels of burthen, the least water being 3 fathoms over the flats opposite the river Talagos.

Between the Noones and the Pongo, the coast is covered with small islands and shoals, extending 3 or 4 leagues from the land, and another bank 4 leagues West of the Pongo, therefore coming from Rio Noones keep outside all, approaching no nearer than 7 fathoms until the mouth of the river is open, when you may haul in and anchor at the entrance in 4 fathoms. There is ample room inside the bank, but as the distance is not materially greater it is considered more prudent and safe to keep outside. The land along this coast is marshy, intersected with creeks and rivers, and extremely low, excepting the mountains of Cape Verga which may be discerned 15 leagues off, and serve as a mark for that Cape.

Rɪᴏ Pᴏɴɢᴏ as well as that of Noones is celebrated for its abundance of ivory and an extensive trade; it is easy of access for vessels from 12 to 14 feet draught, and has commodious and sheltered roads; the winds are generally between the North and West, and the tornadoes blow from the E.S.E. From Rio Pongo the coast lies about S.E. 11 leagues to Tumba Point, between which are the rivers Kalkungee, Dembia, and Dania, navigable for small vessels, and much frequented by the Portuguese for ivory, &c.

Off Tumba Point are the isles de Loos, Tamara or the largest to the West; Factory Island to the East, (about 3 miles from the Point) and Crawford's Island between the two, with two or three smaller ones to the South. These islands are excessively commodious for trade being most easy of access, and commanding a communication with the variety of rivers in the vicinity of the coast; the principal anchorage is on the East side of Factory Island, half a mile from the shore in 4 and 5 fathoms, which excepting during the tornado season (April and May) is safe and good, but at that period the squalls blow directly on the shore, you are therefore entirely dependent on your anchors and cables for safety. The only dangers about here are Cooper's Rocks, and Crawford's Flats, the former is half a mile South of Shark Island, which you are clear of, when Coral Island is open with the South point of Factory; the flats are 1 mile and a half North from Crawford's Island, they are a mile in breadth and dry on the outer edge at low water, in every other respect the channel through the islands is perfectly safe. The tide rises 13 feet and flows with a N.E. moon. The West end of Tamara is in 9° 25′ N. lat. 13° 27′ W. long. Coming from the North it appears like a tract of land, rising with a gentle acclivity on both sides, to a moderate height towards the centre, it is covered with wood, and bold close to the shore on the North side. Good fishing may be found about all the islands with the seine and an abundance of turtle, with good fresh water being acquisitions to the numerous other advantages these isles possess. From hence the Sangaree Mount or Volcano is to be plainly seen in a N.E. direction over Dembia; and it may be useful to observe to the navigator, that North of the islands from the Gambia the soundings are all sandy, and change immediately to mud on the South, which will operate as a criterion for his guidance by night.

From Tumba Point to Matagong Island it is 7 leagues S. E. by S. forming a deep bay between, at the extremity of which are the two rivers Quiaport and Burria, navigable only for small craft, but much esteemed places of trade. On the South side of Matagong is the river Kissey communicating with the Mandingo country, by numerous creeks and branches; it has only 2 fathoms at its entrance as well as Sama river, which is South from it 7 miles, but be careful in avoiding the bank which extends 6 miles from the shore as far as Parrot Island, at the entrance of the Scarcies which is 7½ leagues from Matagong.

From the South side of the little Scarcies there is a bank running out W.N.W. 2½ leagues, tapering away to the Southward as far as Leopards Island, at the mouth of the river Sierra Leon.

The entrance of the river Sierra Leon (called by the natives the Tagrim or Ritomba) is formed by the above island on the North, and Cape Sierra Leon on the South, distant from each other 7 or 8 miles N. by E. and S. by W.; the Channel at its embochure is in a great measure obstructed by an extensive sand bank called the middle ground, which in many parts is dry at low water, but having on each side a passage, the Northern one for small vessels, as far as Tagareen Point, and half a mile from the shore in 2 and 3 fathoms. The one to the Southward between the Cape and the middle ground 2½ miles broad, with from 4 to 13 fathoms. Vessels bound hence from the Westward ought to endeavour to keep rather to the Northward of its parallel, gradually edging down (on attaining soundings) to make the high land, which is a chain of mountains extending to the Southward, when ascertained run in for the highest Peak or Volcano until it bears S.E. by S. bordering on the Cape side, there being no danger but the Carpenter, which is a half-tide rock three-quarters of a mile West of the Cape, between whence and the Cape the passage is clear, and may be adopted in cases of great emergency. The outer edge of the middle ground bears North from the Cape which is the only invisible danger here; between it however and the South shore there are regular soundings all the way to Farran Point. In working up or down do not approach the bank nearer than 7 fathoms. From the entrance there are 4 bights or bays on the starboard shore, viz. Cape Bay, Pirates' Bay, White Man's Bay, and St. George's Bay, where the English have established a Settlement, having good anchorage in 10 fathoms abreast the Fort.*

---

* This Colony was first established by the English Government in the year 1786. under the direction of Captain Tomson of the navy, who took with him 400 distressed Negroes from London, with about 60 Whites to cultivate and clear that proportion of country, which was ceded by King Tom for the purpose of colonization, this system however soon failed, which induced Mr. Thornton, Mr. Wilberforce, and other intelligent members to undertake the object on a different plan, who justly conceiving, that very little benefit could accrue from the mere abolition of the Slave Trade; without the natives being instructed in the principles of religion, and the arts of civil life, which alone can render them a free people; suggested a better digested mode of action, and in consequence sent out new colonists in the year 1792, when an eligible town was erected containing two or three hundred houses and Governors' apartments. In the year 1794 the French very illiberally sent out a squadron which almost levelled every thing to the ground ; however any similar incursions are amply provided against

From George's Bay steer East, until Tagrin Point bears North, and you are in 7 or 8 fathoms, from whence you may stand directly up the river about N.N.E. keeping the West side of Tassa Island open on the starboard bow, which will lead you clear of the bank on its south side, the Channel is then clear as far as Bence and Mitombo Islands with 4 or 5 fathoms, where vessels may lie advantageously for commercial purposes, as a communication exists between this river and the Scarcies, through creeks and over land, the distance of which is not in some parts more than 5 or 6 miles.

Cape Sierra Leon is in 8° 30′ N. lat. and 13° 10′ W. long. with a Westerly variation of 15° 30′ the tide flows on full and change days at 8_H 15′ with a rise of 12 feet ; during the rains it runs with incredible velocity, and the ebb sets strong on the middle ground.

On this part of the coast as far as the Rio Grande, the Harmatan generally prevails about the month of January, continuing sometimes without intermission for a fortnight, this is succeeded by regular land and sea breezes until February, when the winds commonly set in from between the North and West. The tornadoes begin to make their appearance about the close of March, continually occurring until May, when the rains set in, and are almost incessant all July and August, abating in October, and are succeeded by a recurrence of tornadoes ; the winds during the rainy months are for the most part from the Southward and Westward, with boisterous squally weather at intervals.

A Description of the Coast from Sierra Leon to Cape Mount.

From Cape Sierra Leon to the False Cape it is 7 miles S.S.W. and from thence to Cape Shilling 22 miles S.S.E. a little Easterly, keeping about a league and a half out to clear the Turtle Rocks and other smaller ones in shore; the chain of the Leon Mountains runs as far as Cape Shilling, with a graduated descent to the Cape,

---

for the future ; and it is to be hoped their laudable and benevolent labours may be ultimately crowned with every success, though much is to be feared from the rigour of the climate.

which is low, covered with trees, and at 4 leagues distance appears like an island: two and a half miles West of it there is a moderate sized rock above water, and a sunken one called the Wolf, 4 miles W.S.W. from the Cape, which you avoid by keeping over to the East point of Banana, which is an island of submarine volcanic production, about a league and a half in length and only one mile broad; its East Point lies 10 miles from Cape Shilling, with two small islets on its West side, which are surrounded by rocks. The most preferable anchorage is on the North and South sides. The Western extremity, or the islets, are in 8° 2′ North, and 13° 10′ West, being due South from Cape Sierra Leon. From Cape Shilling it is 7 leagues S. by E. to Tassa Point, forming Yawry Bay, which shoals to 3 or 4 feet two leagues out, and covered with productive oyster beds.

Two leagues W.S.W. from Tassa Point are the Plantain Islands, and a smaller one half a league called Skinner, between which and the former there is a channel for small vessels, with a good sheltered anchorage under Rocky Point, in 2 fathoms, otherwise the Plantains are encompassed with shoals that extend 3 leagues to the West, with a ledge of rocks, called the Bengals, and 2 leagues to the North, which must be avoided by keeping 5 fathoms round.

West of this coast are the great shoals of St. Ann, lying in a N.E. and S.W. direction towards the Cape of that name; the broadest part is 8 leagues across, with very irregular soundings all over, from 8 to 2 and 3 fathoms; the North end is in 8° 10′ North latitude, and 13° 36′ West longitude, from whence they run 12 leagues in a Southerly direction, then S.E. as far as the Cape; the Eastern extremity is 13 miles from the Banana islets, between which is the direct channel to the River Sherbro.

The River Sherbro's entrance is formed by Tassa Point and the Turtle Islands, which are 5 or 6 in number, lying N.W. from Cape St. Ann, the Westernmost being 5 leagues distant.

Sailing Directions for the River Sherbro.

Coming into Yawry Bay from the North, steer due South from
the East end of the Bananas, taking care to approach no nearer the
Plantains than 5 fathoms, or a league and a half, to avoid the
Bengal Rocks; and when the West end of Plantain bears E.N.E.
steer S.E. by E. as far as Pow Grande, which is known by several
high trees on the North point of Sherbro Island; in passing the
Plantains, however, take notice of the Turtle Bank, which is small
but of hard sand, and only 5 feet on it, bearing S. by W. two
leagues and a half from the West end of the Plantains. From
Pow Grande keep along shore in 5 or 6 fathoms, to avoid the bank
of the middle ground, until you come to Jenkins, where there is
good anchorage, and is the general rendezvous for trading vessels
of large draught; if a small vessel and bound up to Bagroo River,
steer N.E. between the banks until abreast of Bagroo Point, from
whence keep the larboard shore on board to the creek : if bound to
York Island, steer from Jenkins between Bob's Island and Jamaica
Point, until you open Cuckold's Creek on the starboard side, then
steer for the West point of Large Island, keeping along its South
shore until the East end of it bears N.N.E. then stand over for
Cuckold's Point, and from thence S.E. to the anchorage on the
North side of York Island, where there are from 4 to 5 fathoms
good bottom. From York Island you may sail out of the River
Shebar to the South in small craft.

On the West side of the Turtle Islands there is a channel over
the great shoal, called the Swash, one mile and three-quarters in
breadth, and not less than 3 fathoms all through.

CAPE ST. ANN, is the Western extremity of Sherbro Island,
stretching to the West in a very low point from a moderate eminence
inland; it lies in 7° 8′ North latitude, and 12° 36′ West longitude,
a N.E. moon makes high water with 11 feet rise. From the Cape
to Manna Point, the East side of the River Shebar, it is 8 leagues
S.E.; some high land is to be seen from hence in the interior,

but the coast is low but covered with wood down to a sandy beach. From thence it is 5¼ leagues to the River Gallinas, at the mouth of which, there are shoals and a spit of sand, rendering it only accessible for small boats. From Gallinas to Cape Mount it is 16 leagues S.E. by E. between which there are two small rivers, Mana and Sugary, with good anchorage off the former, in 8 fathoms, during the fine season only.

The Windward Coast.

That proportion of the Coast of Africa that has, by custom, received the appellation of the Windward Coast, extends from Cape Mount to Assinee; and is divided into three distinct countries, particularised from the production peculiar to each, and are most commonly known by the Grain Coast, the Ivory Coast, and the Coast of Adau, or Quaqua.

The winds and weather all along this tract of country are very much similar; if any variation, the rains commence a little earlier as you advance towards the S.E. The winter months in these regions, generally speaking, make their appearance early in June, by strong breezes and occasional heavy gusts from the Southward and S.E. accompanied with rains, that increase with violence and continue until the latter end of August, this is succeeded by a series of close foggy weather, during which the land appears enveloped in vapour, occasioned by exhalations from the earth, which has been so plentifully saturated with humidity during the rains; and from fatal experience, is justly considered to be the most inimical and pernicious season to the European constitution, in the year; the whole atmosphere, at that time, is impregnated with a superabundant quantity of deleterious matter, generated by decayed vegetation, a considerable proportion of which must be inhaled in the operation of breathing.* During the rains there are no land winds, neither

---

* Since the unhealthiness and diseases peculiar to the Coast of Africa are much augmented and provoked by the unconscious imprudences of European visitors, it may not be deemed superfluous to venture a few hints relative to the preservation of health, whilst under the influence of its climate; which, without aspiring or pre-

in the month of October, when the wind is strong *down* the coast, and in the following month gradually draws round to the South and Westward, with occasional rain : towards the middle of December the weather begins to clear up, and the summer months make their appearance, which continue until June, with a beautiful clear sky and gentle refreshing breezes from the S.S.W. during the last ten or twelve weeks of which, the tornadoes prevail very violently ; they come on generally towards the evening, giving ample warning to the navigator to prepare against their incredible impetuosity. The tornado derives its appellation from the Portuguese, it is a corruption of the word trovado, a thunder storm, and is a phenomenon that particularly prevails on the Coast of Africa, from the

---

tending to the skill of medical science, are merely offered as the result of observation and experience.

In the first place, exercise, which is so generally avoided and considered unnecessary under an Equatorial sun, is assuredly more essential, than can possibly be imagined : from hence is not, however, to be inferred, injudicial exposure to the sun, or violent and indiscriminate exercise, but a constant and moderate activity of body as well as of the mind ; which the author has generally found to contribute largely towards the support of health.

Secondly, moderation and regularity in the habits of eating and drinking, form a very material branch in the system to be adopted ; the plainest food is strongly recommended, with care to avoid the use of fats or oils of every description, which act as a powerful stimulus to generate a superabundance of bile, from whence are known to originate numerous causes of fever. The baneful effects arising from the free indulgence of spirituous liquors, need scarcely be expressed, however, thirst being a prevalent sensation in a warm climate, and nature, in some measure, requiring occasional supplies to assist the operations of perspiration, the following beverages are recommended as the most wholesome : good brandy, hollands, or light wines, plentifully diluted with water ; and totally to explode the use of malt liquors, which (though it is almost a general practice to drink in hot climates) are excessively pernicious.

Lastly, it is deemed most important to avoid, with peculiar care, sleeping in the night dews, or exposition to them with an empty stomach at an early period of the morning, during the exhalation, when they rise from the earth impregnated with various dileterious qualities ; and are the more dangerous from the remarkable susceptibility of the stomach in an empty state ; in which case the use of bitters with a biscuit, immediately on rising, will serve to repel their violent effects.

In ships, frequent fumigations of tobacco or pitch, ought to be practised in those parts that are inhabited, and occasional smoaking may be recommended to the crew, as very efficacious in the expulsion of corrupt matter from the surrounding air.

River Noones to the River Danger, but are most severely felt on the Windward Coast; it, however, seems provided by the wisdom of Providence to expel the quantities of obnoxious matter with which the air is so frequently charged, and it is impossible to convey to the minds of those who have not witnessed this wonderful meteor and its effects, a sufficiently accurate idea of it; it first announces itself by the appearance of a small silvery cloud in the zenith, which gradually increases and descends towards the horizon, and becomes veiled over with the most impenetrable darkness; at this moment the functions of nature seem to be paralysed and the elements to have ceased their operations; the most profound and solemn stillness reigns around, with scarcely a breath of air from the heavens, in consequence of which the whole physical system feels oppressed with sensations of approaching suffocation; violent and reverberated peels of distant thunder and lightning commence, gradually advancing and increasing to an extreme not easy to describe, the atmosphere being, at times, in a continued blaze for minutes without intermission; at length the gust arrives with, sometimes, the greatest irresistible violence, the impulse of which no sails can frequently withstand: it is fortunately not of long duration, extending from one to three hours, and concludes with a furious deluge of rain, that descends rather in columns than in drops. The great danger is in the sudden impulse of the gust, which would immediately dismast or overturn a vesssel unprepared for the event. Nothing can be more exquisitely delightful than the subsequent clear and pure state of the air, creating an apparent regeneration of the animal as well as the vegetable world. There is another periodical wind peculiar to this part of the world, called the Harmatan, which blows from the East, and prevails occasionally in the months of December, January and February; it commonly appears three or four times within the three months, continuing from seven to fourteen days, and extends from 10 to 20 leagues off shore, blowing sometimes a fresh top-gallant breeze, accompanied with a thick haze, which increases as you approach the shore, where also the qualities which characterize it are more powerful in their effects; it possesses a peculiar tendency to absorb all moisture, materially

G

affecting every thing of wood, opening the seems of ships, decks, casks, &c. and is particularly destructive to vegetation ; it is excessively pernicious to the organs of vision, conveying with it a considerable quantity of red sand, which sometimes will colour the sails ; it chops the face and parches up the lips, but is favourable to all cutaneous diseases, and appears, from strict analysis, to be the Syroc of the Mediterranean, only less violent in its effects.

The current on this coast, generally speaking, runs with great rapidity to the Eastward as far as the Bight of Biaffra, where it is met by another, which runs along the Southern coast to the North. They change, however, their course in an opposite direction, during the rains and the strong winds that precede that season, and sometimes on the full and change of the moon. Near Cape Mount it sets in upon the shore, and on the West side of Cape Palmas, about a point from the shore, running with considerable violence round the Cape.

From Cape Mount to the River St. John.

Cape Mount lies in 6° 44′ North latitude, and 11° 34′ West longitude, by a good chronometer, with 20° 40′ Westerly, variation ; it is a high promontory projecting into the sea, and may be seen at a distance of 12 leagues in fine weather, it is very remarkable and easily recognized by its cliffs, 4 leagues distant.

Coming from the Westward at night, without having previously seen the land, it is essential to take the precaution of occasionally sounding, on account of the current, which sets with considerable velocity towards the Cape, where there are 15 fathoms close in shore, therefore ought not to be approached nearer than 20 or 25 by dark. During the occurrence of the Haramatans, the sun is for days too obscured by haze to admit of meridional observations, rendering, thereby, your latitude, by dead reckoning, uncertain, on account of the prevalent currents ; in consequence of which, the approach to Cape St. Ann, or this vicinity, exacts the strictest precautionary measures and attention of the navigator, at the same time I deem it necessary to enjoin him not to confide in the navigation per charts, all of which, hitherto published, are decidedly erroneous, and most particularly those of the African Pilot.

On the N.W. side of Cape Mount there is a river of the same name, and is much celebrated for the activity of its trade ; between the mouth and the Cape, there is good riding in the bay, in from 6 to 15 fathoms during the fine weather, but anchorage in 12 to 14 should be preferred in the rainy months, where it is even hazardous to lie, unless provided with the best ground tackle, for at that period, the Southerly and S.W. winds set into the bight, with a most tremendous sea and heavy gusts, producing a violent surf on the beach.

From Cape Mount to Cape Monserrado, the coast lies S.E. 44 miles, the land is all low with a white sandy beach; and 10 miles N.W. of the latter Cape is the river St. Paul's, only navigable for boats, but before which there is good anchorage in 10 fathoms, two miles off.

Cape Monserrado is a high point of land with a gradual declivity into the sea, towards the South, and an abrupt and perpendicular descent on the North, which renders it easily distinguishable from Cape Mount. In the year 1816, the author observed the South point in 6° 14′ North, and 11° 26′ West, with 21° 0′ Westerly variation. When the Cape bears N.E. it assumes the appearance of an island, with groves of trees rising out of the water to the North ; to the N.W. there is a bay, where a ship may come to in fine weather, two miles off shore, in 10 to 13 fathoms, the point bearing S.E. by S. but in the winter months, here as at Cape Mount, vessels should lay well out, on account of the heavy sea in the bay, and the Southerly winds, which otherwise render it excessively difficult to get to windward out of the bight.

It will be useful to observe, that from Cape Monserrado to Cape Palmas may be coasted down in the night with the greatest safety, by keeping the lead going occasionally, and not approaching nearer than 20 to 23 fathoms, when you will be from 4 to 6 miles from the shore ; it is safe even much nearer, but as there is no inducement nor any object to be gained by closing in the night, it is considered more prudent and advisable to keep at a safe distance, in which case you will have sufficient time and room to obviate any inattentions of the helmsman diverging from his course.

By day the land is in fine weather distinctly seen off deck, 20 miles distant, when you will be in about 50 or 55 fathoms, which last circumstance may serve as a guide on approaching this coast during the night.

About 8 leagues S.E. by E. from Cape Monserrado lies the river Junk, discovered by a remarkable saddle hummock some distance in the country; in fine weather about 2½ or 3 miles from the shore there is good anchorage with a clean sandy bottom in 12 fathoms, at the following bearings, the entrance of the river North, with the hummock N.E. It must be understood that in the rainy season, a greater distance is required to be taken for anchoring at the different places on this coast, on account of the wind setting strong towards the shore. Six miles to the Westward there is a small reef, but not very dangerous as it is close in shore, but there are some sunken rocks on each side the river's mouth, which boats ought to avoid by keeping amid-channel; good fresh water may be procured here, and it being a scarce article on this coast, ships if in want should embrace the advantage, taking care to send sufficient protection for their boats against the treachery of the natives.

Twelve miles S.E. from the latter river there is a small town called Picanniny Bassa, remarkable for a large conspicuous house, the residence of the Chief. Abreast the town there is a dangerous ledge extending 5 miles to the S.E. with foul ground about, and renders it necessary to anchor no nearer than 15 fathoms, with the large house N.E. by E. and the nine trees E.S.E., which latter lie 5 miles to leeward, on an eminence above a considerable habitation called Bulham Town; they form a principal feature for the guidance of navigators on this coast, being distinctly seen at a great distance; from these trees to the river St. John it is almost 4 miles, this river forming the Western limits of the Grain Coast; on each side of its entrance there is a small town; it is only accessible for boats, and the inhabitants here are more tractable than at the former places.

From St. John's the large town of Grand Bassa is about 2 miles down the coast; there is good anchorage with muddy bottom in 12 fathoms, the nine trees bearing N.N.W. a very large cotton-tree on the beach E. by N. and other large spreading trees at Tobacconce S.E.; there is a small river below the town, at the mouth of which is a small but commodious cove for small craft, with from 2 to 6 fathoms, bounded on the West by two large rocks, between which and the shore a vessel of 14 feet-draught may moor with safety, in cases of great emergency.

Seven miles S.E. by S. from Bassa Point is Tobacconee known by its four or five immense trees and a very large rock, with which is connected a sunken reef extending as far as Poor River; there is however a clear passage for trading boats between it and the shore.

From Grand Bassa to Cape Palmas the ground is all extremely foul and rocky, and where small working chain cables prove of essential use, particularly to mercantile vessels that are obliged to come to, almost at every place of trade.

On the System of Traffic or Barter pursued between Cape Mount and Grand Bassa.

On account of the strong current which prevails along this coast to the S.E. vessels bound hence for trade most commonly commence to windward, and progressively run the coast down to their last place of destination, and as the more important branches of commerce are comprehended between Cape Mount and the River Danger, the former naturally becomes the first point of visit or resort, for otherwise much time is unnecessarily lost to the navigator, and expense as well as demurrage incurred on the merchant.

It is customary on your arrival off the coast first to signify your intention to trade, by firing a gun and hoisting your colours, on doing which the natives will come off and communicate the articles they have for sale, or if too late in the evening to venture off they make large fires on the beach, which is a signal that they wish to trade; should you have reason to suppose there is any inducement to stop, it will be advisable and indeed necessary to come to an anchor, otherwise the traders will all go on shore again.

It is also essential to intimate to strangers in this commerce, that the greatest possible patience and forbearance is requisite, to treat with the inhabitants particularly of the windward coast, who will immediately desert you on the slightest manifestation of violence or direct opposition.

At the various towns you will always find natives to go certain distances down the coast in the characters of interpreters and mediators, they prove of great use sometimes, and are recommended in proportion to their different merits by certificates or books as they term them from the masters of various trading vessels, but are nevertheless not at any time to be implicitly depended upon. Their expenses are trifling as you pay them in common articles, at the rate of 18*d.* sterling per diem.

The whole trade of this coast constitutes merely a simple system of bartering one article for another, and commences with what is termed the bar trade from Cape Mount to Bassa, an appellation that has originated in the value of all merchandise, being estimated at so many bars of iron, and as every article has its stated valuation it renders this traffic comparatively simple; the regulated prices being as follow with the variety of articles that are most suitable and in demand.

Ivory is the staple commodity procured in exchange about here, as well as a fine species of Camwood, of which there is generally a great abundance at Cape Mount, but from the many acts of treachery that have occurred there, it may be recommended to traders not to send boats on shore excepting in very necessitous cases, and then well armed; neither to trust any quantity of goods with the natives without a proportionate guarantee for there being accounted for; if they possess ivory and are in any way anxious to trade, they will readily come off in their canoes providing the vessel comes to in the bay.

A LIST OF ARTICLES MOST ADAPTED TO THIS TRADE.

Example of Purchase
for a Tooth of 40lb.

	Bars.
1 Blue Baft	9
1 Piece of Rowal	6
1 Niccanee	8
2 Guns	12
4 Iron Bars	4
50 Flints	1
2lb. of Tobacco	4
10 Kegs of Powder	10
2 Iron Pots	2
2 Bottles of Rum	1
2 Worsted Caps	1
2 Looking Glasses	2
	60

All Manchester Cloth.

Bars.	
9	Blue Bafts
8	Nicanees
6	Romals
10	Bijudaponts
10	Chilloes
6	Khali Ghillies
6	Tom Coffees
6	French Guns
6	Tower Guns
2	Brass Pans
2	One Hundred Flints
3	Box of Pipes
2	Tobacco per lb.
1	Iron Pots
2	Rum per Gallon
96	Barrel of Powder
1	Measure of ditto, made to contain one pound
5	Cochetes, 10 yards
1	Worsted Caps, 2
1	Trade Hats
1	Iron Bars
1	Looking Glasses
	Crockery Ware of all Sorts, Jugs, Mugs, Plates, &c. &c.

(Per Piece)

You must not be surprised or alarmed at the exorbitant exactions of the black merchants, who without discrimination, will at first make most unreasonable demands ; however the mode of bartering is thus : The owner of the tooth of ivory will ask so many bars for it, which the purchaser must gradually abate until he obtains it at such a rate as may enable him to make a reasonable profit, which can be easily estimated by comparing the invoice prices of the goods, and the price of ivory at home, in addition to which ought to be considered the expenses of freight and interest.

All teeth under 22lb. are termed scrivelloes, and may generally be procured at a much lower rate, also for the most trifling articles. Monserrado is commonly well stocked with fine teeth ; the inhabitants are also quiet, and tractable, and you may go to their residence up the lake with the utmost safety, where they receive you with kindness and hospitality, observing the greatest possible respect, combined with the most honourable integrity in the course of barter; but previous to commencing, a customary douceur of brandy must be proffered as a stimulus to commercial operations.

Junk varies very much in its supplies, sometimes having none, at others in great abundance, but Bassa is scarcely ever without, from the incredible droves of elephants that frequent the surrounding countries. As in every other part of the world the prices of articles are influenced by the demand and competition, which if great will frequently cause a sensible loss in the purchase; therefore vessels trading down the coast should particularly avoid following each other too closely, a circumstance that must inevitably mar the prospects of both.

Description of the Coast from Grand Bassa to Cape Palmas.

Seven miles S.E. by S. from Bassa Cove is the large Tobacconee Rock, recognized by a clump of spreading trees over the town of that name, connected with the rock there is a sunken reef, extending as far as Poor River, with a passage between it and the shore for small trade boats.

From the Tobacconee Rock to the river Sesters the land lies S.E. about 10 leagues, between which are five towns on the beach, namely Young Sesters, Piccaniny Sesters, Grand Currow, Timbo, and Manna, besides a few straggling residences on the West side of the river. Grand Currow is known by a high hill inland, called the Tobacco Mount, and the latter town by a clump of high ruddy colored trees; it is a rocky coast, with a very foul bottom, as is the case all the way to Cape Palmas, in consequence of which a light working chain cable is deemed serviceable and economical, having such frequent necessity to come to an anchor at the different trading places.

RIVER SESTERS is in 3° 34′ North latitude, and 9° 46′ West longitude, it is navigable for boats 5 leagues up, as far as King's Town, but covered with rocks at the entrance, two miles from the shore, some of which are above water. The river may be recognized by a chain of three hills inland, one of which is much smaller than the rest, and you can anchor abreast in 10 fathoms muddy bottom. From hence to Sanguin it is nearly 6 leagues, in the same direction, with a small town between called Rock Sesters, known by its large solitary palm tree on the point, and a little to the Westward of the river, a large rock with a bushy clump on the top, half a league from the shore, called the Devil's Rock. From Sanguin to Settra Krow it is 12 leagues S.E. ½ S. with six intervening towns, Baffoo, Tassoo, Battoo, Snow Hill, Barbara, and Krowba, which are of inconsiderable note, therefore unworthy of further detail, than to observe, off Snow Hill the anchorage is good in 16 fathoms, sand and stones, 1½ league from the shore; it is known by a large tree standing on the extremity of a Point.

SETTRA KROW is a very large town, but the ground excessively foul and dangerous to anchor, the rapidity of the current being so great.

It is on this part of the coast you may hire men to assist the ship's crew in the more laborious occupations of trade; they are strong, willing, hard-working people, and strongly recommended to the oil vessels bound to leeward, as being extremely serviceable in cases of emergency, or sickness of their own men: they are faithful to you in a strange country, and content with a small dash, or present, on quitting at the Islands of Princes or St. Thomas, from whence they commonly find conveyance back to the coast. From Settra Krow to Rio dos Escravos it is 8 leagues, steering S.E. as far as Krow Settra (which is 3 leagues) to avoid a reef of rocks that runs out a couple of miles, and then S.E. by E. to Drou, at the entrance of the above-mentioned river: off Wappau, which is 2½ leagues from Krow Settra, is the Swallow Rock, bearing nearly S.W. 2½ miles from the town, and S.S.W. 3 miles from Flat Island; between this island and Krow Settra, there is good anchorage in 10 to 15 fathoms, sandy bottom; and the latter place is rendered remarkable by the number of high bare trees seen at a great distance. The Town of Niffoo is 4 miles from the river, both of which places were formerly celebrated for the quantities of slaves they furnished; hence the river is called Escravos, or Slave River, which is small and only navigable for boats.

From Drou to Cape Palmas it is 15 leagues, S.E. by E. between whence are the towns Little Sesters, Baddou, Grand Sesters, Garraway, and Rock Town, of which Grand Sesters is the most considerable, being a very large numerously inhabited place; it is foul on the West side with a high rock about two miles and a half to the Southward. Garraway is known by three hills, with a clump of trees on the Southern extreme point.

H

In doubling the Cape, it is essential to be cautious of the two dangers that exist off it ; namely, the reef or shoal which lies nearly 3 miles to the South, and a sunken rock, called Coley's Rock, (upon which are only 6 feet and breaks in high winds) 6 leagues, the pitch of the Cape bearing N.E. by E. and the trees on Garraway, North a little West. The current on the West side sets with great rapidity to the S.E. about a point from the land, rendering it necessary, in sailing round, to keep within the direct course to prevent being set out from the land.

Mode of Traffic from Grand Bassa to Cape Palmas.

The system of barter established between these two places, is termed the round trade; a round is a nominal mode of valuation, and signifies one of every article employed in this traffic, and is thus performed ; For a tooth of ivory, the vender will demand so many rounds according to the value he affixes to the tooth, and as there are no established prices, he is induced to ask very exhorbitantly for, in which case the purchaser can only be guided by the sterling value of his own goods, and thereby calculate what proportion he may give, in order to ensure a profit; then, as many rounds as are agreed upon, he is to give as many pieces of cloth, flints, kegs of powder, guns, hands of tobacco, &c. &c. as per example ; a piece of cloth, one fathom in length is termed a short piece, and three fathoms a long piece; and half the number of rounds the tooth sells for are to be long, and the other half short pieces, if an odd number, it is to be an additional short piece ; also if it is a tooth of eleven rounds or more, one whole piece of blue baft is to be given, and counted as one long piece. (as in purchase No. 2.)

As it would prove too expensive to give an equal number of guns as rounds; two, three, or more may be given, according to the size of the tooth, and the remainder substituted by tobacco, two hands of which equal (or room) a gun.

The same articles as for the bar trade answer, with the only addition of Neptunes which are highly prized, and in great demand. Brass pans, however, will occasionally substitute them.

A keg of powder contains about half a pound ; seven leaves of tobacco make a hand, and seven hands go to the pound.

For a tooth of four rounds give two long and two short pieces : for five rounds give two long and three short pieces : for six rounds three long and three short pieces : for seven rounds three long and four short pieces and so on. Small scrivellas of two, three, or four pounds may be had for pipes and tobacco; more or less guns will be required according to the competition.

EXAMPLES OF PURCHASE.

No. 1.   No. 2.

For a Tooth of 29lbs. six rounds.	*For a Tooth of 45lbs. eleven rounds.*
3 Fathoms of blue baft *(one long piece)*	1 Blue baft (one long piece)
7 Ditto of Romal { two long and three short pieces.	1¼ Piece of Romal } four long and six
	4 Fath. of Nicceance } short pieces
1 French gun	1 French gun
1 Brass pan	1 Tower gun
1 Iron pot, 6 flints	18 Hands of tobacco, to room 9 guns
1 Cap and 1 pint mug	3 Hands ditto, for trade bunch
6 Kegs of powder	2 Brass pans (one to room a Neptune)
10 Hands of tobacco, to room 5 guns	11 Kegs of powder
2 Bottles of rum	1 Iron pot, 1 cap
10 Pipes	2 Spans of iron bar (each span contain-
2 Spans of iron bar	ing 8 or 9 inches)
	2 Bottles of rum
	6 Pipes and 1 trade bat.

The production of this part of the coast is principally ivory, Malagatta pepper and rice ; the last of which may be obtained in great quantities and grown to any extent, provided encouragement is given by the demand ; for it is now little cultivated on account of its being little called for ; the species is excellent, but the natives not possessing the art of properly cleansing it, it appears to great disadvantage.

Description of the Coast from Cape Palmas to Cape Lahou.

Between these two places is comprehended what is termed the Ivory or Teeth Coast, being distant from the former 42 leagues, E.N.E.

Cape Palmas is the Southermost point of Guinea, it is moderately high land, thickly wooded, with small hillocks and cliffs towards the sea, intersected with red clay fissures resembling tracks, or roads, and a large mud walled town on the Easternmost elevation. It lies in 4° 25′ N. lat. and 8° 13′ W. long. with 22° 40′ Westerly variation.

To Cavally River it is 5 leagues, with a small intermediate town called Grooway. Cavally is situated on the right bank of the river, on the opposite side of which, is a reef of rocks running out a considerable distance from Steep Point; the river is accessible for boats some distance up, taking care to avoid the ledge above-mentioned.

Hence it is 6 leagues due East to Tabou Point, which is very low and flat with heavy breakers on it; the anchorage is good here in 15 fathoms two miles off.

From Tabou to Tahou the distance is 11 leagues, with considerably higher land than before, being varied with many hummocks. There are four intervening towns namely, Bassa, Buttrou, Wabbou and Bereby, between which two latter is the river Poo.

Three miles South from Bereby, is a large conic rock, called the Devil's Rock, and a ledge connected with it and the shore.

Tahou is a large sized town, half a league West of the river, before whence you have good riding, in 12 or 14 fathoms, taking care no to come too near the rocks West of the town.

It must be remarked, on this side the Cape the bottom is principally muddy, sand and clay.

From Tahou to St. Andrew's River it is 11 leagues, and the coast very recognizable by the high land of Drewin which stretches along 3 leagues towards the river, terminating near Swarton corner, with two large round topped trees on the summit. The land abreast the river forms a sort of bight or bay where there is an excellent road, in from 8 to 12 fathoms, fine sandy bottom, the two trees bearing N.W. by W.; from the anchorage are seen three high hills about 15 miles inland, appearing in one when the river is open, and East of the river a line of red cliffs extending 12 miles, which enable the navigator to distinguish this place with facility; you may go up the river 6 or 7 miles in boats, where there are a number of towns with very dangerous and treacherous inhabitants; on, entering take care of the black rock in the middle; good water may be had in abundance 2½ miles up on the starboard side.

From St. Andrew's it is 11 leagues to Rio de Lagos, which place is by some considered the Eastern boundary of the Tooth Coast; from Rio de Lagos the land stretches E. by N. 6½ leagues to Kotrow, and then E. by S. 10 leagues to Cape Lahou.

On the Trade of the last mentioned Places.

The mode of barter to Cape Lahou is the round trade, as before, varying in a few points from Bereby to the Cape; viz. the long pieces are from three to four handkerchiefs and the short ones two; also ounce and half ounce powder kegs are made use of, the former containing 14lbs. but valued in proportion.

Cape Town, Grooway, and Cavally produce an abundance of rice and grain of all rorts; at the other places as far as Lahou principally ivory is to be had, with an incredible abundance of palm oil, if the natives will collect it; more or less ivory will be found according to the occupations of the traders; therefore vessels should make a point of trying all the towns, and not pass by any, from the circumstance of a former voyage producing little or none, for by so doing traders have frequently lost opportunities of making extensive purchases. St. Andrew's and Lagos river are most commonly well stocked.

Description of the Adou or Quaqua Coast, from Cape Lahou to Assinee.

Cape Lahou lies in 5° 17′ N. lat. and 5° 20′ W. long. with a town of great magnitude and extensive population, on the larboard shore of a small river of the same name; from which to Jack Lahou and river, it is 4½ leagues East, and thence to Piccaninny Bassam 8 leagues E. by N. ½ N. with the intermediate towns of Wattoe and Jaque Jaques. Abreast of Piccaninny Bassam it is steep, close to the shore, having 140 fathoms 2 miles off; from which circumstance the bay has received the appellation of the Bottomless Pit; therefore vessels wishing to trade here should come to, a few miles to the Eastward where there are only from 30 to 35 fathoms sandy bottom.   Eight leagues E.S.E. from Piccaninny Bassam is the river Cesta with the town of Grand Bassam on the right bank; opposite there is good anchorage in from 9 to 12 fathoms, 2½ miles off, with the river open mud and clay bottom.   Plenty of refreshments and water may be had here, and is exclusively a place of great trade.

From Grand Bassam the coast lies about E. ⅓ S. 6¼ leagues to the river Assinee, which place is difficult to discriminate unless well in shore, on account of its being shut in by the immense high bushy trees around; the town of Assinee that formerly stood on the beach, was destroyed in 1814, by the neighbouring hordes who are jealous of the extensive trade usually carried on; the land is particularly low about here, but the trees very high, which at the mouth of the river appear at a distance with an opening at the top, resembling the intervening space between two neighbouring woods visible considerably far off.

The current is excessively rapid here to the Eastward, and you anchor abreast the river in 10 and 13 fathoms, sand and clay, half a league distant.   The river is navigable for trade boats many leagues up, extending itself 20 miles from the entrance into a large lake, contracting again into its former width; upon the banks are many towns that have constant communication with the gold country in the interior; it is a place seldom visited, for want of knowledge by some, and by many passed by, since the destruction of the town, which was the principal leading mark.   The inhabitants are extremely timid and require encouragement to give them confidence. Formerly there was a French garrison and fort on the river, but the natives jealous of their power obliged them to abandon it in the year 1706, and demolished their fortifications.

The rains along this part of the coast set in towards May.   The produce of oil here as well as on every other part of the Gold Coast is profusely great.   The season for which commences in September, after the catoon custom or harvest home.   The trade is in many respects similar to that of the Gold Coast as far as the river Volta, and will be treated of hereafter.

Description of the Coast from Assinee to Cape St. Paul's.

The intermediate country of these two places forms what is termed the Gold Coast, on account of its abundant production of that metal.

The seasons are precisely similar to those of the Windward coast, with the exception of their successively commencing a month earlier; in the winter season along this coast when the winds are from the S.W. the swell and surf on the beach are excessively high and dangerous in many parts to attempt landing.

From Assinee to Gold River it is 6 leagues E. ½ S. a low thickly wooded country, with the small town of Albanee on the beach about half way. On the West side of Gold River stands the town of Tabo, where there is sometimes great commercial activity, but the river is inaccessible. Vessels should be particularly careful in not approaching too near this part of the coast, it being excessively shoal to two leagues out, with an indraught and heavy surf on shore.

From Tabo to Cape Appolonia it is 4 leagues on the same course, between which the land begins to rise with an undulated assemblage of hills and hummocks, four of which predominate, forming a line along the coast, and render it particularly remarkable coming from the Westward; they are interspersed with a variety of clumps of palm trees.

The Cape lies in 5° 00' North latitude, and 3° 24' West longitude, 4 miles from whence on the beach is a British fort and settlement. The landing is very bad, and dangerous to cross the bar, in consequence of which the natives take you from your boats in their canoes; the anchorage also is very inferior, the most preferable however being at the following bearings: the fort N. ½ W. and the body of the Cape N.N.W. ½ W. in 13 or 14 fathoms.

From Cape Appolonia to Axim it is 6½ leagues E. by S. the town stands on the East side of the Rio Cobre, where there is a Dutch fort and factory, near it are some rocks in shore, with a good landing place inside; great supplies of gold are to be had here sometimes, as at Appolonia. You may anchor in 10 fathoms, the fort

N.N.E. To the West side of Cape Three Points it is then 5 leagues, with another Dutch fort near the Cape, called Brandenburgh Castle, which is of inconsiderable note. Cape Three Points is a promontory of land so called from its presenting to the sea, on the South side, three projecting Capes or Points of land, lying parallel with each other, East and West, 3½ leagues distant between the extreme Points; it is moderately high, even land, bold but excessively rocky all round, with two sandy bays between the Points. The current is extremely rapid in this vicinity, and frequently sets directly on the Cape, with a great rippling, which renders it necessary to steer wide accordingly.

The course from Cape Palmas, is E. ½ S. 126 leagues, but it is necessary to keep within it on account of the current, which setting to the Southward might carry you from the land, and to leeward of your destination. The middle Cape (which is the point of calculation) lies in 4° 41' North latitude, and 2° 55' West Longitude, with 23° Westerly variation, a league to the Southward of which is a dangerous sunken rock, which it may be recommended to give a good birth to in passing. The reef mentioned by Dalzel as lying outside does not exist.

The town of Tacramah is between the West and middle Points, and the Dutch fort of Arquidah on the beach of the East Point, abreast both of which you may anchor in 14 to 24 fathoms, three or four miles off. Four leagues from Acquidah is another English fort called Dixcove, it is a commodious resort for trading vessels, being well situated for interior communication, on account of its being adjacent to the great path to Tuffero and Warsaw; it possesses abundant supplies of refreshments, wood and water; on each side the fort are many sunken rocks, forming between a species of roadsted, and shelter for trade boats, with a good and convenient landing place. Large vessels should anchor in 16 fathoms, the fort bearing North. Between Dixcove and John's River, there are five other forts, namely: Bautry, Tacorady, two at Secondee, and Chama. The environs of Tacorady, are extremely rocky and about a league and a half to the Southward of it there is a considerable and dangerous shoal that generally breaks, and in the night must be avoided by keeping in 16 fathoms outside ; be careful not to come too near, particularly in light winds, as the course of the current rather inclines towards the breakers. The Fort of Chama stands about 4 miles on the West side of the river St. John's, which is navigable for small trading craft nearly 20 miles up, where an extensive traffic for gold is carried on.

On the East side about 2½ leagues are situated the two English and Dutch Forts of Commenda, known by a little mount to the left, called Gold Hill. The coast is rather foul about the forts, and you must not approach nearer than 9 fathoms, when the anchorage is very good with a sandy bottom, the British Fort bearing N. W.

Nearly 8 miles E.N.E. is the principal settlement of the Dutch, called St. George del Mina, which is defended by a handsome well constructed and powerful fortification, situated on the beach, and supported by a second fort on a commanding eminence behind, called Mount St. Jago, the whole commanding a very formidable and beautiful appearance from the sea; hitherto the establishment has been much neglected by the Dutch, and the garrison frequently reduced to seek supplies and assistance from the adjoining British settlements. To the right of the fort there is a small river where coasting craft may shelter or haul on the beach in cases of emergency, for repair, &c.; large vessels anchor in 9 fathoms, sand and mud ; the fort Flag-Staff bearing N.W. 2 miles.

Three leagues and a half to the Eastward is the principal British settlement of Cape Coast, defended by a castle or citadel on the beach, but far inferior to the former in point of strength or beauty, it is conducted by a company who are allowed annually to the amount of between twenty or thirty thousand pounds for defraying all expences of that and the adjacent subordinate forts.

To the left of the Castle there is a small conic hill, called Phipp's Mount, on which formerly existed a square tower, but is now totally mouldered into dust ; the best anchorage therefore is half a mile to windward of the Citadel, in 7 fathoms, sandy bottom, and Phipp's Mount well open to the West of it ; the old roads abreast the Fort, according to Dalzel is by no means recommended, being excessively foul.

t

Cape Coast is badly supplied with water, and chiefly depends on the quantities collected in tanks (constructed for the purpose) during the rains which generally commence about the latter end of May, and continue with unabated vigour for a period of six weeks; there is a pond near the town from whence the natives offer to furnish vessels, but is extremely pernicious, and advised not to be accepted; for the Governor will always accommodate if possible all ships in necessitous cases. The Castle lies in 5° 2′ North latitude, and 2° 3′ West longitude.

The trade of this part of the coast is very variable, sometimes extremely active, at others equally dull, depending greatly on the back countries for the supplies of gold with which they abound, and which are not brought to the coast regularly, if the natives are engaged in war. The Ashantees, a powerful nation behind, have recently succeeded in obtaining a direct intercourse with the Whites, which circumstance it is to be hoped may lead to various commercial advantages, as well as an enhancement of our local knowledge and discoveries in the interior.

The climate in the vicinity of Cape Coast is by no means so unhealthy as in many other parts; the period however most pernicious to Europeans is from June to September, during the rains and exhalations, which may be avoided by running over to the Portuguese islands for residence until their expiration.

Two leagues and a half from the Castle is the small Dutch Fort of Nassau, with a chain of the Cormantine mountains, inland to the right, between it and the British Fort of Anamaboo, which is 4 leagues from Cape Coast; you may anchor before it in 7 or 8 fathoms, the Cormantines open to the Eastward of the Fort; the Dutch have another factory situated on a hill, 2 leagues from hence to the right of the Cormantine river, which with the last-mentioned place furnishes an abundance of provisions and refreshments at a more moderate price than to windward, and have sometimes a great proportion of gold for sale ; to Tantumquerry Point it is then 5 leagues East, the coast is bold all along, and you may keep close in to 8 and 10 fathoms, from John's river to windward to the Rio Volta ; one league round Tantumquerry Point there is a British Fort which is generally considered a good trading place, and you may anchor before it in 9 fathoms; the next fort and settlement is Dutch, 3 leagues E.N.E. called Apam, but is now abandoned, as is the case with all the Dutch settlements to the Eastward of Accra. Three and a half leagues farther is the town of Whinebah, where the British had a strong fort, which was destroyed in the year 1812, on account of many acts of violence committed by the natives on the Governor and Settlers. Between Apam and this place is a moderate sized hill, called the Devil's Hill, which serves to recognize these places. From Whinebah there is a communicating path to the large commercial town of Kibbes, in the country of the gold mines, and to the Eastward, a river which furnishes good water if taken sufficiently far up, otherwise it is powerfully brackish : there is good anchorage abreast the town in 7 fathoms, the Devil's Hill bearing N.W.

Three leagues from the latter place is another Dutch abandoned Fort, situated very conspicuously on the declivity of a thickly wooded hill near the Point called Barracoe, and which is known by two distant hills to the Northward, called the Paps: coming hence give the fort Point a birth, on account of some rocks that lie round it.

Six leagues farther East, on the West point of the river Saccoom is a small hill called the Cook's Loaf, with the town of Saccoom on the East side, from whence to Accra it is 3 leagues; the land in this vicinity is loftier than to windward, with the high Tafou gold mountains to be seen behind.

Accra is an extensive and considerable place of trade, containing several factories, besides three distinct forts situated in a line along the coast; the first is St. James, British ; the second, Creve Cœur, Dutch ; and the third, Christianburgh Danish. Large quantities of ivory are frequently found here, as well as an abundance of gold which the natives manufacture with the rudest implements into a variety of beautiful trinkets, with extreme neatness and ingenuity ;

The neighbouring country presents an agreeable and varied prospect, with more than usual indications of cultivation and amenity; it is scantily supplied with water, but abounds in a profusion of game, with all sorts of provision and stock, particularly an excellent species of Indian corn which may be obtained in great abundance, at the rate of two shillings and sixpence a bushel.

The surf here is frequently very heavy and high on the beach, consequently the landing bad, and the anchorage foul outside, excepting when St. James's Fort bears due North, in 8 or 9 fathoms, where you have very soft clay, which renders it necessary to come to, with a light anchor, as it is almost impossible to extricate a heavy one when once immersed in the clay; in fine weather vessels may lie much nearer in shore in 6 or 7 fathoms, good sandy bottom.

From Accra to Ningo river it is 10 leagues, E.N.E. with three intervening forts, Temah, Danish, 4¼ leagues distant; Poney, Dutch, but abandoned, 2 leagues farther; and Prampram, British, 1½ league; all of very inconsiderable note and little trade. From Ningo river and its vicinity may be easily distinguished the celebrated Crobo mountains, at a considerable distance inland, the highest of which, towers much above the rest in the form of a sugar loaf, called Ningo Grande. On the right bank of the river is a fine large fort and settlement belonging to the Danes, which is easily known by a line of small hills to the Eastward: the anchorage between Ningo and Prampram is generally speaking good in 6 to 9 fathoms, gravel and sand.

From Ningo the coast is almost on a level with the sea, as far as Sandy Bluff, the West Point of the Rio Volta, to whence it is 10 leagues, E. by S.

Rio Volta, so named by the Portuguese on account of its rapidity, lies in 5° 52′ North latitude, and 0° 40ᴸ East longitude, and and takes its source in the Crobo country, running in a S.S.E. direction to the embouchure, which to vessels coming frum the Westward does not open until it bears N.N.W.; it is half a league wide at the entrance, with an island a short distance up amid-channel, on which is established a strong Danish Fort; the river is navigable for vessels of 9 or 10 feet draught to a considerable distance beyond the island, but particular care and attention ought to be observed in entering.

The West point is called Sandy Bluff, and the East, Woody Bluff; from the former there runs a bank and heavy breakers, in a S.E. direction more than half way across, consequently sailing in, keep on towards Woody Bluff in 3 or 4 fathoms, from whence you may stand into the river, along the East shore as far as Aoonah Creek, having from 10 to 12 feet water abreast the fort.

The trade of this river was formerly very great, but of late years for want of its acquaintance and other causes, has been little frequented although immense quantities of ivory are procured by the neighbouring inhabitants, who now carry it to the Popoe country for disposal. Before the river there is a large bank extending to the S.E. about sixteen or eighteen miles, formed by the bodies of sand and mud that are ejected from its bed by the prodigious velocity of the stream.

From Rio Volta it is 5 leagues to Cape St. Paul's, with very low broken land, forming the Eastern extremity of the Gold Coast. The Cape is a very low projecting point, lying in 5° 50′ North latitude, and 0° 37′ East longitude, and is easily distinguished as the land trenches away to the N.E.; a league to the Westward of the Point is the entrance of Dry River, which runs along the coast 2 or 3 leagues inland, communicating with the Popoe Lake and the country of Whydah.

A Description of the Mode of Traffic employed from Cape Lahou to Cape St. Paul's.

The system of barter that prevails between the above-mentioned places is nearly similar, and is termed the ounce and ackey trade, from the circumstance of every article of merchandize being estimated at so many ounces or ackeys of gold, the former of which is the ounce troy, and the latter the sixteenth part of an ounce; consequently every thing having a stated price tends very much to sim·plify and facilitate the exchange of goods; there is however one material thing to be observed, which is the variation of price in goods when given in exchange for gold or any other article.

The gold prices are liable to vary, but those of trade are regular, and established as under :

Articles of Barter.	Ounce.	Ackey
Barrel of Powder	3 to 8	
Long Dane Guns		9 to 10
Mock Dane ditto		6
Tower ditto		6
Double iron bars		6
Single ditto		4
Red Taffeties		2
Flints per hundred		
Brass Pans	2	
Pipes per box		3
Glasgow Danes, 8 Handkerchiefs		8
Cupidas		
Quadruccas		
Bonny Blue Bonals		4 to 10
Red Niccanees		8
Blue ditto		6
Blue Bafts		6
Bijudaponts		6
Pholas		8
Pondicherry Romals		10
Rum, per 5 Gallon Keg		10
Trade hats		8
Scarlet Cloth per fathom		6
Striped Silks		6
Ginghams		8

The cloths for this market must, generally speaking, be India, and those of the finest nature; for the extreme nicety of the black merchants in their taste and choice, surpasses that of the most scrupulous and refined London tradesman: Powder is commonly a principal article of barter, but experiences a material variation of price, which is influenced by the supplies on the coast, or the demand in the interior, Guns are very desirable, which, to command the markets, ought to be of the best quality of Tower and long Danes. Neptunes are much liked in the vicinity of Cape Lahou, as well as a species of pipes, called the Cape Lahou pipes; and Portuguese tobacco will be found in great demand all along the Gold Coast. Traders to the Gold Coast cannot err if they take a good assortment of fine India romals, taffeties, ginghams, striped silks, common scarlet cloth, and any thing rich colored, which are highly prized by the Ashantees, and natives of the back countries.

The principal articles to be had in return are ivory, gold, palm oil, gums, and pod peppers. Gold in great profusion at Cape Lahou; and at Jacques·Jacques unbounded productions of oil, which is of excellent quality; the whole of this neighbourhood is entirely wooded with the palm tree, and the natives desirous of collecting it, but hitherto the demand has been very circumscribed, and the place little resorted to for that article, excepting by coasting vessels; otherwise there is no doubt but the trade would become very formidable.

Assinee should never be passed by: with encouragement it will be found a desirable place of trade, the inhabitants up the river have it in their power to procure large supplies of both gold and ivory; but on account of many predatory attacks from Spanish slave vessels, they are excessively timid, and with difficulty are persuaded to bring it off until they have gained sufficient confidence. Appolonia (as at all the other forts) the trade is almost monopolized by the white residents, who purchase up all the produce and re-sell it to the vessels. The Caboceer, however, is immensely rich, and will oftentimes make very extensive purchases, but is rather difficult to deal with though strictly honorable. The greatest supplies of gold most commonly come to Cape Coast from whence there is a constant intercourse, either directly or indirectly, with all the inner countries where that metal is generally procured. The forts to leeward of Cape Coast also furnish considerable quantities of gold and ivory, particularly Accra where it is advisable to touch. The whole of the neighbouring country (which is extremely fertile) has recently been cultivated to a very considerable extent, and is now become celebrated for the produce of maize, or Indian wheat, which may be procured in any quantities at the rate of two shillings a bushel from the natives, and three from the factories, which latter is preferable on account of the time that is saved in the purchase, unless merchants pursuing this trade establish factories, which is still more desirable.

It must be remarked to those who wish to pursue the African barter with any degree of success, that from the extreme versatility of taste on the part of the natives, the most punctilious observance to the choice and demands respecting the various articles of sale, is of the greatest possible importance. The trader ought consequently, on quitting the country, to pay every attention to the then state of the market, and make his notes preparatory for an ensuing voyage, of such merchandize as he may deem most requisite for another season; for what is quite the rage one year will the following one, most probable, be rejected with the greatest disdain. The quality of your merchandize should be good to ensure any advantage over your competitors.

Description of the Coast from Cape St. Paul's to Cape Formoso, constituting what is called the Bight of Benin.

The seasons on this part of the Coast are nearly similar to those of the Gold Coast; the rains commencing early in May, which are preceded by the tornadoes and boisterous squally weather, with Southerly and S.S.E. winds from the month of March, causing a heavy sea in the Bight, with a violent surf all along shore. The finest months are from September to March, during which the winds are from W.N.W. to W.S.W. with cool refreshing breezes by day, and land winds at night. But, take notice, in the bad weather and the winter months, there are no land winds, and the current is frequently found running rapidly to windward; which observation applies to the whole of the West Coast of Africa.

The land from Cape St. Paul's runs about 14 leagues in a N.E. direction, then nearly five degrees East, as far as the kingdom of Benin, from whence it trenches S.S.E. to Cape Formoso, forming the great Bight.

The country as far as Wydah is called the Slave Coast, from the incredible numbers of slaves it furnished during the pursuit of that traffic, principally coming from the dominions of Dahomy and Fouin.

From the Cape to Quitta, it is 4½ leagues N.E. with the intervening town of Awey, 3 leagues to Acquijah, and 2¾ to Paurey in a similar course, with a flat coast all the way; it is then 4½ leagues to the town of Gugligou, known by the four hills which lie in the vicinity near the shore, and 6½ leagues to Little Popoe, a town where formerly was established a Dutch factory: you may anchor before the town, bearing North, in 7 to 9 fathoms, sandy bottom;

there is a small river commucicating with the lake behind, but rendered inaccessible by a bar of mud and sand that has choaked up the embouchure.

From Little to Great Popoe it is 10 leagues E. by N. a low swampy country : there are three towns or factories, formerly in possession of the English, Portuguese, and Dutch ; the natives of which still speak the different languages, and are severally governed by Caboceers or Chiefs, who style themselves of the country, to which each factory formerly belonged. The houses are well constructed and generally two stories high with stone steps. There is a good market with the most abundant supplies of stock of every species, and a diversity of fruits the most delicious. The natives and chiefs are respectful, honest, and desirous of trade. Ivory abounds here in endless quantities, which is constantly sent from the inland towns to the Northward by corresponding traders to the coast; few vessels call here which makes them tractable and easy to trade with. The ounce and ackey system still prevails, with pretty nearly the same assortment of goods as to windward, viz. striped silks, cuttanees, bandanoes, Manchester fancy romals and long cloths, but valued upon an average 20 per cent higher than to windward, and ounce kegs of powder containing 20lb. are used.

The mode of proceeding is thus on arriving, it is necessary to go on shore, (for the natives will not bring their trade to the ship) with samples of each of your articles of merchandize, and pronounce before an assembly of the Caboceers their various prices, which you must maintain as high as possible, (though obliged sometimes to abate.) When the prices are agreed on, by both parties, a piece of cloth and a few gallons of rum are paid to each Caboceer, for custom ; upon which you open trade.

The owner of the tooth of ivory sells it through the medium of a broker, who according to its size makes a demand, which never fails to be exorbitant, however you must patiently abate until he reduces it to a price you can afford to give; observe, that independent of the assortment that is given, the broker on commencing will desire you to hold back a certain number of ackeys in proportion to the size of the tooth, which are afterwards to be paid to him.

K

POPOE like Accra, possesses inexhaustible quantities of the Indian wheat obtainable at a very low rate. It is a place that merits the attention of vessels, being a very superior port of trade.

The bar being bad with a high surf, occasionally requires a little attention on the part of strangers, as to the time of landing.

From Great Popoe E. by N. 5 leagues, is the town of Wydah, a low marshy coast, with an exception of a small hill, half-way, called Mount Palaver, which with two very large round topped trees to the right near the sea, serve as a good leading mark for the town, abreast of which there is a convenient road in 7 or 8 fathoms, muddy bottom, 2½ miles from the shore, the town of Wydah bearing N. by E. and the two round topped trees N.N.W.

From Wydah it is 10 leagues E. by S. to Porto Novo, with two intervening towns, called Jackin and Appee, the former 5 and the latter 6 leagues from Wydah.

PORTO NOVO is the sea-port of the capital of the kingdom of Ardrah, which lies 5 leagues inland, to the Northward, and has always been in the habit of supporting an active trade if encouraged: you may anchor in 7 fathoms abreast the town, a heavy clay ground; hence to Badagry, a small inconsiderable residence, it is 5¼ leagues and from thence to Lagos it is 12 leagues E. ¼ S. along which coast it is low uninhabited, and thickly wooded with palm trees, which naturally supposes the possibility of deriving great sources of oil from hence.

What is generally called the mouth of the river Lagos, forms the entrance to Cradoo lake, which extends nearly 15 leagues East, having many towns on its shores, the principal of which is Cradoo, where the Jaboo cloths are to be had in plenty and of fine texture; the lake is a couple of leagues across the widest part ; and is connected with the river Formoso, by many creeks navigable for the country canoes. On the left of the entrance to the N.W. are the rivers, West, Lagos and Doo; the second of which extends in a W. by N. direction near 60 or 80 leagues, taking its source in the kingdom of Fouin and Ardrah, from whence abundant supplies of produce are conveyed.

The town of Lagos is situated on the North side of an island, just within the mouth ; the town is large, thickly inhabited, and carries on a very extensive commerce, both with the interior and on the coast, with principally Portuguese vessels. The entrance, coming from Porto Novo is easily recognized by a town and a large spreading tree, called the Monkey Tree, on the East point, which you must bring to bear N.N.E. with the river open to obtain the best anchorage in 7 fathoms, called English road, where large vessels commonly come to.

From the West to the East point it is about three-quarters of a mile, with projecting banks of mud and sand on each side ; the one from the East point stretching to the S.W. which renders the channel rather contracted, and only navigable for very small vessels, there being little more than 5 to 7 feet at low water; the passage however up to Lagos is on the N.W. side of the island, keeping close to the shore, where you have 7 or 8 feet, and will avoid the Pelican bank to the left, which dries at ¼ ebb; the tide rises and falls about 5 feet, and it is high water on the full and change, at 5½ʜ   English Road is in 6° 13′ North Latitude, and 3° 1′ East Longitude, with two points Westerly variation. What is called the French Road is about 5 miles farther to the Eastward, from whence there is a path over-land to communicate with Lagos. From the month of March when the strong breezes set in, and during the rains it is necessary to be particularly careful in entering the river, for the sea is then prodigiously high, and breaks with violent surfs on the beach.

From Lagos the coast runs with a slight curve to the Eastward, as far as the small town of Palma, 10 leagues distant, low swampy country, with an extensive sandy beach ; thence to the town of Oddy, it is 9 leagues E. by S. with a few straggling huts about half-way, the sandy beach still continuing nearly 7 leagues farther, where there is a remarkable high spreading tree, with only 4½ fathoms abreast. To this tree you may run all the way from St. Paul's, by the lead in from 7 to 9 fathoms, when you will be about 1½ league from the shore.

From the tree the coast trenches away S.E. 3 leagues to a small fish-town, with several intervening clumps of high trees, and from thence to the N.W head, (which is the left entrance of Rio Formoso) it is 7 leagues the same course, with low bushy wood in front of a thick row of trees of regular height, a sandy shore and several isolated houses at long distances, with only 4½ and 5 fathoms, 2 leagues off, and 3½ abreast the river.

Coming from the Westward to Benin, strangers are advised to keep on a parallel of 6° North, and make the land about the large tree, standing along shore from thence to the N.W. head ; otherwise they may over-run their distance, and get off some of the rivers to the Eastward, which it is extremely hazardous to enter without being well prepared and defended.

The Benin River or Rio Formoso, has since the abolition of the slave trade been totally deserted, and is now very little known or frequented. The natives never on any account come outside the bar, on which account many vessels being off here with a desire to trade, and not seeing the canoes appear as to windward, have again left it with the idea that no trade existed in the river.

The N.W. head lies in 5° 34′ North latitude, and 4° 55′ East longitude, with 24° Westerly variation, the tide flowing at 6 on the full and change, with a rise of 5 or 6 feet. The chart draughts of the river are found very inaccurate and defective.

The best anchorage outside for large vessels is about 4 or 5 miles from the bar in 4½ fathoms, the river well open and the N.W. head N.E. by compass in heavy mud and clay.

On the East side of the entrance there is a small assemblage of huts called Salt Town, from whence to the N.W. head it is 2½ miles with a broad bar stretching across to a distance of one mile outside, on which there is never less than 12 feet in the deepest part (or East side) at low water, and 15 or 16 at high water; on the West side there is a sandy spit running to the S.S.W. which in some parts dries at low water, and is very dangerous to approach too near, for the sea commonly sets directly over the bar with great impetuosity, the waves rolling in continued succession and with frequent breaks, particularly when the winds are in the least fresh. Sailing in, stand

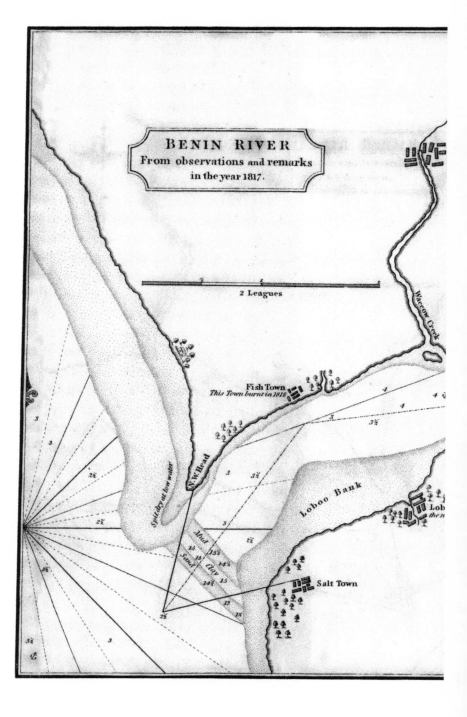

BENIN RIVER
From observations and remarks
in the year 1817.

2 Leagues

Waccow Creek

Fish Town
This Town burnt in 1818

N. W. Head

Spit dry at low water

Loboo Bank

Lob
the n

Mud
Sand
Clay

Salt Town

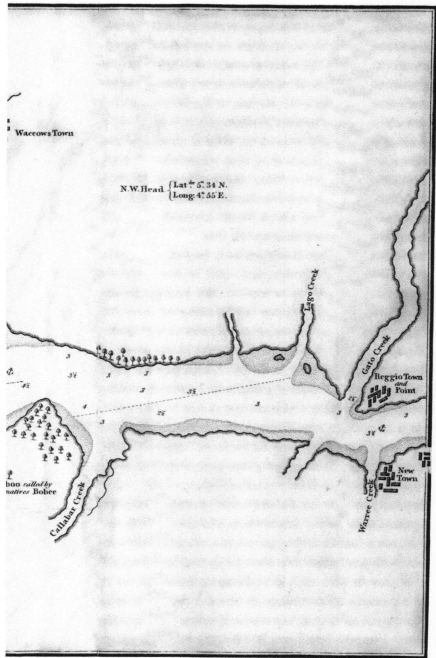

Waccows Town

N.W. Head. { Lat^{de} 5°. 34 N.
{ Long: 4°. 55' E.

Lago Creek

Gato Creek

Reggio Town
and Point

boo *called by*
natives Bobee

Callabar Creek

Warree Creek

New Town

Engraved by W. G. Rowe.

towards Salt Town Point until within half a league, and the N.W. head bears N. by E. when steer N.E. by N. over the bar in the direction of a small town, called Fish Town* on the larboard shore, to avoid the Labou bank opposite the town of that name, and which nearly reaches two-thirds over; when abreast of Fish Town in 3½ fathoms, you will see a Bluff Point 2 leagues up on the larboard side, known by its remarkable projecting tree, and is called Jo Point, for which you must steer, where there is anchorage in 4 fathoms amid-channel; on the opposite shore is a creek (with a small island at the mouth) leading up to Waccow's Town, 5 miles distant.

Round Jo Point you will see a creek called Callebar Creek, and another small inlet farther up on the larboard side, called Iago Creek, with two small islands at the entrance, and a mud bank running out a quarter of a mile from them, to avoid which, keep on the starboard shore, and when pas the islets cross over to the large opening, called Reggio, or Gato Creek, where you may anchor abreast the town of Reggio, on the left, or New Town, on the right, in 3½ and 4 fathoms. The latter is the sea port town of the King of Warree, and the residence of a governor, who is a representative of the king. The Caboceer, or head governor of the river, lives at Lobou ; called Bobee by the natives. Gato Creek leads up to a considerable town of the same name, which is the commercial port of the King of Benin, another powerful chief; it is 14 leagues up, but only navigable for trade boats, which, however, may carry on a very extensive and profitable trade in ivory.

From Reggio Point to Formoso is navigable for many leagues farther in an E.N.E. direction, but unnecessary for present commercial purposes, as the points of communication with the chiefs of the two dominions, are confined to the two aforesaid towns.

---

* This town in March of 1818, was expressly burnt, being represented to the king by his fettish men, or necromancers, as a necessary step to appease the Deity who had deprived them of trade so long: in consequence the inhabitants received an immediate mandate to seek some other abode, and it was sacrificed in solemn pomp, together with a hog and bullock, whose blood was strewed across the river by the principal chiefs, followed in splendid procession by all the natives in their war canoes, and the females dressed in white, uttering cries and songs appropriate to the occasion.

For vessels intending to remain any length of time in the river, the most advisable anchorage is abreast of Jo Point, where they are open to the sea breezes, and in a central situation for all trading purposes. The Loboo Governor makes a point of boarding every vessel that enters the river, in obedience to the strict injunctions of the king, who is tyrannical to an excess.

It may be prudent to suggest to those who intend to frequent this river, the necessity of their vessels being well manned and armed, to provide against the treachery of the natives, and particularly the chiefs, who have more than once seized upon vessels, and appropriated the cargoes to their own purposes.

Rio Formoso, during the fine months, is extremely healthy, being perfectly open to the sea breezes, with a free draught through the roads.

Mode of Barter at Benin.

The produce to be found in this part of the country is ivory, pod pepper, and palm oil, which latter is procured in the greatest possible abundance, all over the dominions of the King of Warree; they receive in exchange the different articles mentioned hereafter, every one of which has a stated valuation in pawns, a nominal mode of value, whose origin is quite unknown.

The small East-India shell, or cowry, constitutes the currency of the country, and coral beads, the intrinsic treasures of the rich, being held in the highest estimation, and from the rarity, is only in the hands of a few chiefs, whose avidity for them is immeasurable; the species admired are the pipe beads of various dimensions, and are valued at ten large jars of oil an ounce, of the smaller sort, and so on in proportion for the larger sized.

The cloths, for this trade are principally of Manchester manufacture, and those most preferred are the handkerchief pieces, generally of light patterns. Black silk handkerchiefs and chintzes are much prized, also Brazil tobacco, which is expressly prepared for this market, is in great demand. Spirits will be found here a very desirable and profitable article of sale.

The measures principally in use, are the oil jars, which are of two sorts, of the largest containing about four gallons, and the smallest not quite three; for powder a small half-pint mug, and for salt a mess kid, or crew, made to contain five pounds.

There is a difference to be observed in the payment for the oil, to the king, who has one and a half pawn for the large jars, and one pawn for the smallest, whilst the people only receive one for the former, and two pawns for three of the latter. These prices are only recently established, and may be maintained with facility by the observance of a little decision towards them, but if deviated from, will totally destroy any advantages that may accrue from this trade.

Pawns.	
1	All Handkerchiefs
1	Long Cloths per yard
	Two Crews of Salt
1	Iron bars
15 to 20	Neptunes
2 to 3	Two quart jugs
1	Trade hats
3	Fine hats
10 to 12	Guns, short French banded
8	Rum, per gallon
4	Brass pans
2	Coral pipe beads
	Cowries
1	Looking glasses
	Manillas
1	Copper rods, two
2	Ginghams
	White bafts (a few desirable)
	Bandanoes, each handkerchief
2	A few copper rods

The large jars contain about 28lb. of oil, and the small ones 20.

Particular attention should be paid to the necessity of giving a regular proportion of articles, so as not to dissort your cargo; say eight or ten handkerchiefs to every twenty large jars, with iron bars, powder, rum, and other small goods to make up the payment; a small quantity of salt may be introduced occasionally which will very much reduce the cost of the oil. On entering the river, vessels are boarded by the two Governors of Bobee and New Town, with whom you send up a deputy to treat with the King of Warree, accompanied with the following comey or custom which he must receive previous to opening trade. Thirty pieces of the most common cloth, six guns, one barrel of powder, a small cask of rum, and a few other small articles.

The same form is necessary for the King of Benin, if you wish to purchase ivory, which is the principal produce of his dominions, and may be had in great abundance, at the rate of three pounds for two pawns, or at most one pawn per pound, for which they take in exchange a quantity of salt with other articles.

The governors above mentioned ought much to be mistrusted and guarded against; at the same time as representatives of the king (who never comes to the river) they must be humoured and encouraged, for their power is very great and almost uncontrouled.*

Waccos Town supplies a quantity of oil as well as ivory, also provisions of all sorts, which are extremely reasonable. The pepper and red wood are of excellent quality, particularly the former, which is obtained at a very low rate. Particular care should be observed in the water that is made use of, it being of a very inferior nature, on account of the swampy state of the adjacent country, however is best some distance beyond New Town, and ought always to be boiled for drinking.

Sailing out of Benin River, if possible avail yourself of the springs, and drop down as far as the bar with the evening ebb, so as to be in readiness to weigh and stand out with the morning ebb, and the advantage of the land wind. The ebb sets down the river towards Fish Town and from thence to the S.S.E. along shore.

Vessels intending to trade to the Southward, should here lay in a stock of Jaboo cloths, which are there greatly esteemed; they are to be had in great quantities, from one to twenty five pawns per piece; some of the best sort are quite equal to Manchester manufacture, but are only made in two or three inch widths. Jaboo carries on a constant commercial communication with this river for cloths, through the medium of various connecting creeks.

---

* There is a yellow man from Cape Coast named Brew, who is more treacherous and dangerous than the natives, and has been accessary to the cutting off and detaining one or two trade boats, and with very great reason suspected of poisoning one of the mates.

The season most favourable for traders resorting to the River Formoso, is between the months of September and the latter end of February, during which period there are clear refreshing breezes with fine weather, and land winds to enable your getting over the bar in coming out; but it is recommended not to remain over the month of February, otherwise much danger and difficulty may be apprehended in sailing over the bar, with the weather that generally succeeds that month.

From Benin bar to Cape Formoso, the coast lies S.S.E. ¼ E. 26 leagues, a low, swampy, unhealthy country, intersected with creeks and rivulets, which variously communicate with Warree, whose king they are subject to. The first is Rio des Escravos, which lies 4½ leagues from the bar of Benin, with only two fathoms at the entrance, and is a quarter of a mile across; it was formerly a great place for slaves, but is now totally abandoned by traders; it unites with the river Forçados which is nearly 3 leagues farther, leading to the town and capital of Warree, and is known with facility by the island of Forcados, just in the centre of its mouth, and another called Poloma close to the shore on the South side; there are two passages, one on the North side, and the other between the two islands, which is the best in 2 fathoms, as far as the town of Poloma 6 miles up; the anchorage outside is in 7 fathoms, the North end of Forcados, bearing N.E. by E. and the North end of Poloma E. by N. ¼ N.; small crafts going in, must avoid the bank that runs out West from the island on the left.

Rio Dos Ramos is 5 leagues from the latter river, which it does not in the least resemble, being not quite a quarter of a mile wide, nor any island in the vicinity. Four leagues farther there is another river of the same size called Dodo, and from thence to the Cape four more of smaller note; on the last of which is the town of Sengma almost enveloped in the trees. The coast all the way to the Cape is excessively low but thickly wooded, and can be descried little more than 4 leagues off, at which distance the trees appear to be standing in the water; the ground is very shallow about the Cape with a heavy muddy bottom, and in 16 fathoms you are out of sight of land, therefore approach no nearer than 8 or 9 in the night.

The true course from Cape St. Paul's hence, is E. by S. ½ S. 100 leagues, but keep a little to the Southward of this course, on account of the current which frequently sets to the Northward of East.

A Description of the Coast from Cape Formoso to Cameroon's River, in the Bight of Biaffra.

Cape Formoso lies in 4° 20′ North latitude, and 5° 55′ West longitude, the land running due East and West as far as Bonny, having six intermediate rivers. There is a small opening or creek about 2 leagues to the Eastward of the Cape, that must not be mistaken for Nun or the first river, which is 6 leagues, and opens when bearing N.E. and is easily known by the two Bluff Points, Cape Nun to the West, and Cape Tilana to the East. This is the only one of the six rivers that is accessible, and where slave vessels frequently lie at the entrance trading; there is a shoal and small rock half a league out abreast the mouth, on which the sea breaks with great violence. From hence to St. John's, or the second river, it is 5 leagues, which opens when bearing N.E. by E. with a small island on which there are four or five spreading trees; the points are bluff on each side the river, the Easternmost one having several spreading trees upon it. St. Nicholas, or the third river, lies 4 leagues from the latter, but does not open until bearing N.N.W. and is not so considerable as the next one, which is 5½ leagues, called St. Barbara, or the fourth river, opening when it bears N.E. by N. with a wide entrance, and a bluff point on the East side. The fifth river, or St. Bartholomeo, is similar in size to the last, running in a direct line to the Northward, and opens when bearing North; on its West side there is a large remarkable tree inclining towards the water, and a bluff head on the East. The sixth, or Sombrero, is the last river, 8 leagues from Bartholomeo, and 4 from Foché Point, it opens when bearing N. by W. with a graduated bluff on the West side. The coast is thickly covered with the mangrove all along from the Cape, with a sandy beach, and stiff clay and muddy bottom outside, in 6 or 8 fathoms.

From Sombrero there is a hard sand bank, stretching out 2 leagues and a half to the Southward, and as far East as Fochè Point, where it is bordered by a line of breakers, in a N.N.E. direction.

The Western extremity of the bank off Sombrero, occasionally breaks very violently, but you may pass it in 5 or 6 fathoms in safety.

Fochè Point is the Eastern side of an island of that name, and about 5 leagues from Sombrero Bluff, forming with Rough Corner, (which is 7 miles across) the entrance into Bonny and New Callebar rivers, the passage into whence is rendered excessively difficult by the numerous rocks and shoals in the vicinity.

About 5 miles to the Eastward of the Sombrero or Fochè Bank, there is another shoal of hard sand, called the Baleur, connected with the former by a bar across the North side, and another on the South, on which there are only 2½ and 3 fathoms at low water, with 3 to 5 between. The principal passage lies over these bars; consequently, large vessels intending to enter, should come to in 4 or 5 fathoms; Fochè bearing North a little Westerly until the proper time of tide.

Sailing in, bring Fochè Point to bear N. ¼ W. and Rough Corner N.E. by N. ¼ N. steering for the latter, which you must keep open on the starboard bow, when over the bars you will be in 8 fathoms, Fochè Point bearing W. by N. ¼ N. and Rough Corner N.E. From hence, if bound to Bonny, which is 4 leagues up on the starboard side, steer N.N.E. until abreast of Jujew Town, then steer N.E. keeping a very large tree on the opposite, or Peter Forti's land just open on the larboard bow, (to avoid the Deadman's Flat, that runs 2 or 3 miles out from the salt country) which will bring you opposite the town in 10 fathoms. If bound to New Callebar, send for a native pilot, who will take you over the flats.

There is another passage between Rough Corner and the Baleur, called the Portuguese Channel, but rendered more dangerous than the former, on account of the two banks called the Middle Patch, and the Eastern breakers; the mark to clear which, is Andony Point, N.E. by E. and Fochè Point, E. by N. steering for the latter to avoid the spit that stretches out 2 miles from Rough Corner. The current outside runs to the Eastward, at the rate of 1½ mile per hour.

The trade of this river has been for a long period confined to slaving, although it yields a considerable quantity of palm oil, and might become a very formidable market for that article with a little encouragement, particularly on the New Callebar side. But on account of the constant state of disunion between the chiefs it would be advisable to lie at the confluence of the two rivers, to have the benefit of a free trade with both parties. The common Manchester cloths suffice for this place with guns, powder, iron, crockery ware, and small articles, with which you may purchase the oil at a very low rate ; neptunes are much in request on account of the salt that is made here.

From Rough Corner to Andony River the land trenches a little to the Northward, and is 9 leagues distant ; the sea breaks abreast the river, which is blocked up by a hard sand bank. From hence with a similar course E. by N. it is 12 leagues to Tom Shot's Point, which forms the West side of the entrance into Old Callebar River, and is remarkable by a very large spreading tree on the Point, which is not seen until it bears N ½ W. It lies in 4° 24′ North latitude, and 8° 55′ East longitude, opposite which is the East head, bearing E. ½ S. 18 miles.

From Rough Corner to Tom Shot's Point the course is E. ½ N. 22 leagues, which will keep you in 10, 8, and 6 fathoms, and 5 when abreast of Tom Shot, whose shore you must on no account approach too near, or you will not be able to weather the breakers, towards which the flood-tide sets you with great rapidity, the reef is extensive and runs out from Tom Shot's shore to 2 miles South of it ; its extreme point being at the following bearings ; Tom Shot's tree, and point N.N.W. and the East head N.E. a point to the Eastward of which, you will see an opening called Backassy Gap. The breakers extend from the South point in a N.E. direction, about 1½ league, and then break off to the N.W. between 3 or 4 leagues up the Tom Shot's land ; on the S.W. side of them there is a shoal hitherto unnoticed, with only 2½ and 3 fathoms, which renders it necessary not to go to the Northward of the South point of the breakers, but keep well to the Southward in rounding them, if bound for the river.

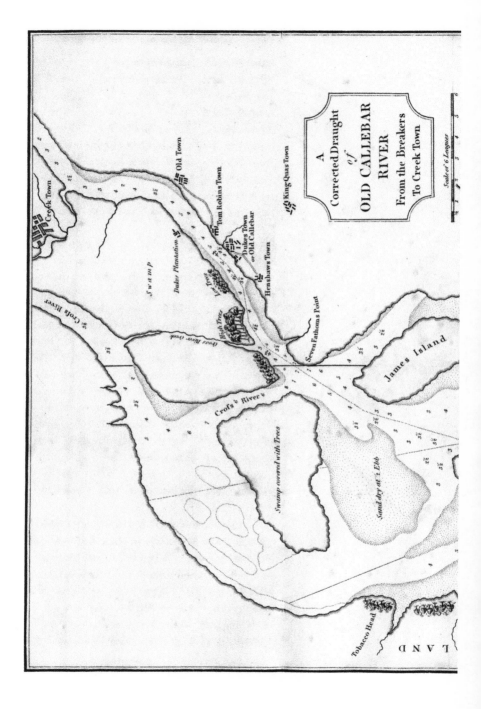

A
Corrected Draught
of
OLD CALLEBAR
RIVER
From the Breakers
To Creek Town

Scale of 6 Leagues

Creek Town

Old Town

Tom Robins Town

Dukes Town
or Old Callebar

Henshaws Town

King Quas Town

Swamp

Dukes Plantation

Low Trees

High Trees

Cross River

Great Bear Creek

Crofs River

Crofs River

Swamp covered with Trees

Seven Fathoms Point

JAMES ISLAND

Sand dry at ½ Ebb

Tobacco Head

LAND

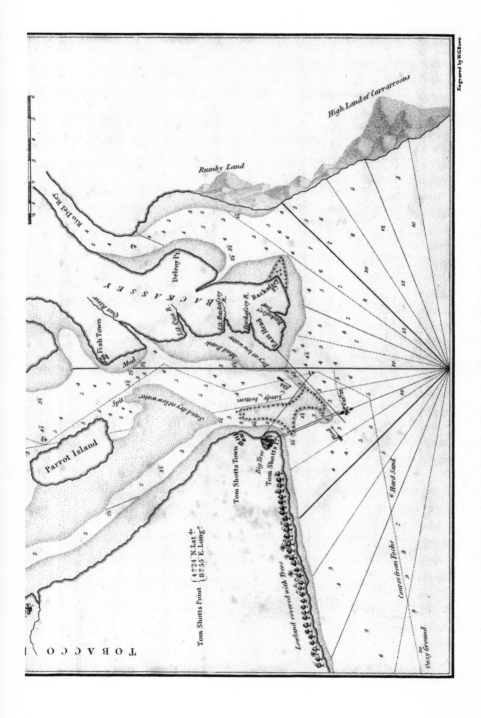

Engraved by W.G.Rowe.

From the East side of the breakers to the East head there is a bar with 3 and 3½ fathoms in the centre at low water, hard sand on the West side shoaling to 2½ fathoms, mud towards the shore of the East head, where in many places it dries at low water nearly a league out, the bank continuing in a due North line, as far as Qua river, between which are the rivers Little Qua, Little Backassy, and Big Backassy. About 4 leagues N.W. from Qua is Parrot island, with a sandy shoal running S.S.E. as far as Qua river, between whence there is but 3 and 2½ fathoms, with a hard spit half-way from Parrot island, which you are clear of when Fish Town Point bears E.N.E.

From Qua River, it is 2 leagues to Fish Town, and from thence 2 leagues, on the same side, to James Island, which extends 4⅟₂ leagues up in a N.N.W. direction, with a shoal of sand on the West side, and a passage between of 2½ fathoms at low water, (called the Flats) one league farther, N.E. by N. on the starboard side is a bluff point, called Seven Fathom Point, which has 6 and 7 fathoms close to the trees, as well as across the channel to Cross River on the opposite side. From Seven Fathom Point the river takes a N.E. by E. direction, with a mud bank stretching half way over the channel, between the Point and Henshaw Town, abreast of which, on the opposite side, is a row of tall trees, with Cross River Creek to the left; on the same side, farther up, are some low bushy trees, near where it begins to shoal; from hence Callebar lies a league up on the opposite side.

Directions for Sailing into Old Callebar.

The breakers, above-mentioned, are both seen and heard at a considerable distance, for the rocks are large and some above water which make a great roaring. When steering for the river's mouth, give them a good birth and stand on to the Eastward, until the East Head bears N.N.E. and the West head, or Tom Shot's Point, bears N.W. when, if it is late in the evening, or ebb tide, come to an anchor, but time and tide favouring, steer North until you bring Big Backassy to bear E.S.E. when you must stand up towards Big Qua River, keeping it a little open on the starboard bow.

Observe that the Backassy shore is mud, and the breakers side, sand; so that when you shoal your water with a soft bottom, edge over to the Westward, and vice versa, shoaling with a sandy bottom, edge over to the Eastward, which rule attended to, may enable you to go up as far as Qua River, by the lead in thick weather.

When abreast of Qua River steer for the East side of Parrot Island, keeping it just open on the larboard bow, taking care to avoid the bank from the Fish Town shore, as well as the bank and spit on the West side of the channel, which is hard sand that dries at low water, but has deep water inside to the N.W. which has entrapped many vessels beating down, by getting within on one tack, and on shore on the other, therefore renders it advisable to caution the stranger against similar errors.

When two-thirds the length of Parrot Island, in 4 fathoms, steer for the North end of James Island, keeping it broad open on the starboard bow, without coming too near the swamp bank, (which in some parts is dry at low water, and is a league and a half from James Island) this channel is shallow, and you will find only $2\frac{1}{4}$, 3, and $3\frac{1}{4}$ fathoms, until you are past the Island, when it will deepen to 4, 5, and 7 fathoms close to Seven Fathom Point, which you must steer for, and from thence to the tall trees on the opposite side, keeping along that shore in 4 fathoms, until you are abreast of Henshaw's Town, situated on an eminence to the right, then stand over amid channel for the anchorage, giving the side from the low trees a good birth, where it is shoal.

The most preferable position for anchoring, is a little to the left of Callebar landing place, in 4 or 5 fathoms, where you will be conveniently situated for trading purposes.

In sailing out of Callebar River take notice, the ebb tide sets with great rapidity out of the Backassy Rivers over the breakers, therefore make all necessary allowances, and as soon as you are over the bar, stand immediately to the S.E. particularly if it is light winds, or you will drift on the breakers, before the vessel can possibly perform any evolutions to obviate difficulties.

Strangers to this river should come to an anchor off the bar, and send up to Duke's Town for a pilot ; but at the same time not to yield to him the command of the vessel as is customary elsewhere, for his knowledge merely consists in that of the channel, without possessing the least idea of the management of a ship.

Merchant vessels are expected to observe the ceremony of requesting a pilot by letter to the Duke of Callebar, the neglect of which, in case of competition may produce disagreeable results.

Although nature is apparently here in a ceaseless state of verdant vegetation, the seasons vary as sensibly as in more temperate regions, contributing to the decay of old and regeneration of new fruits and plants ; the spring commences about the month of November, and continues together with the summer or the hot months until May, during which period the weather is clear and fine, but accompanied with excessive heat and occasional tornadoes. The rains gradually increase from the middle of June continuing all July and August, the latter of which it descends in torrents ; this may be termed their winter, during which, the inhabitants are afflicted with the various diseases most peculiar to them, such as colds, fluxes, fevers, &c. and in September, October, and November, the country is entirely enveloped in exhaled vapour, which the natives term the smokes, and are so decidedly injurious to European constitutions as to be deemed essential if possible to be avoided. Should it prove necessary to remain during this season, occasional fumigations of tobacco through the vessel, together with smoking will be found efficacious in repelling the pernicious effects of the vapour.

Callebar and Cross Rivers are navigable for vessels of burthen, as far up as Creek Town Passage ; and at the breakers the tide flows at 6 on the full and change days, with a rise of 7 feet.

On the System of the Callebar Trade.

The principal produce of this river is palm oil, ivory, pod pepper, and red wood ; the former of which predominates in great abundance, the palm nut arrives at its maturity towards the latter end of February or the beginning of March, sometimes sooner or later, according as the weather may have been favourable or the contrary ; therefore it creates unnecessary loss of time and expense, for merchants to send their ships previous to that period, more particularly so as the occupations of the natives at the plantations totally estrange their attention from the palm oil trade, until, sometimes the end of April.

For the interest of commercial vessels, it is indispensably necessary to observe a great deal of form and ceremony amongst the chiefs, for instance, to salute with two guns off Henshaw's Town, and seven at Duke's Town, with the addition of a formal visit, to announce your arrival to Duke Ephraim, the chief of the place, who holds dominion over an immense tract of surrounding country. By application to him, he will cause the king to go on board the following day to receive his comey or custom, previous to which you cannot commence trade. The comey or customs are exorbitant in this river, and are, as notified in the following table.

COMEY PAID TO THE DUKE AND TRADERS ON ENTERING CALLEBAR RIVER.

DUKE EPHRAIM.

50 Iron Bars
10 Tom Coffees } Manchester.
5 Bonny Blues }
3 Chilloes, 3 Allijars
10 Romals & 3 Pondicherrys
60 Crews of Salt, 3 Umbrellas
1 Box of Pipes, 1 ditto Soap
20 Mugs
70 Trade Hats
10 Caps, 10 Knives
24 Spoons, 3 fine Hats
1 Barrel of Powder
1 Puncheon of Rum
1 Bandana

KING COBHAM.

2 Tom Coffees
2 Bonny Blue Romals
10 Iron Bars
10 Crews of Salt
3 Gallons of Rum
1 Blue Dane
2 Caps

YOUNG KING.

1 Bonny Blue Romal
2 Iron Bars
2 Crews of Salt
1 Gallon of Rum

GEORGE COBHAM.

1 Bonny Blue Romal
1 Gallon of Rum

EYO HONESTY.

3 Bonny Blue Romals
4 Tom Coffees, 1 Hat
3 Quart Mugs, 4 Pint do.
10 Hands of Tobacco
15 Iron bars, 2 caps
20 Crews of Salt
13 Gallons of Rum
15 Kegs of Powder
4 Looking Glasses

ORGAN HENSHAW.

3 Tom Coffees, 6 Iron Bars
6 Kegs of Powder
6 Crews of Salt, 4 Caps
12 Pipes, 4 Pint Mugs
1 Wedge of Soap
12 Gallons of Rum
1 Fine Hat

KING EGBO.

1 Tom Coffee
2 Caps, 2 Pint Mugs
10 Bottles of Rum
3 Iron Bars
4 Crews of Salt

ARCHOBAN DUKE.

2 Romals, 1 Cap
1 Quart Mug
2 Kegs of Powder
6 Crews of Salt

COBBING OFFIUNG.

1 Piece of Cloth
1 Keg of Powder
6 Crews of Salt
1 Cap
1 Looking Glass

KING AQUA.

2 Manchester Romals
4 Kegs of Powder
2 Quart Jugs
5 Looking Glasses
1 Wedge of Soap
4 Iron Bars

EGBO HONESTY.

1 Piece of Sastracundy
4 Iron Bars
6 Kegs of Powder
6 Crews of Salt

JEMMY HENSHAW.

3 Bonny Blues
10 Crews of Salt
6 Kegs of Powder
1 Iron Bar, 2 Caps
2 Pint Mugs
6 Hands of Tobacco

Observe, many other individuals have been on the list, but having ceased to trade, no longer become entitled to receive comey, since the custom was first instituted, for the purpose of giving encouragement to traders.

M

The oil is sent for by the natives of Callebar, Creek Town, and the adjacent residences, to Ecricock, Egbosherry, Aniung, and Little Cameroons, on stated market days, two of which there are per week; the oil is delivered either on board or on shore, in a house which it is the custom to get built for that purpose, and where on arrival you may deposit your empty casks. The price of oil varies in proportion to the quantity, or the competition that exists to obtain it; however it is generally from ten to fourteen coppers per crew, four of which are paid in salt, and the remainder in goods. It is too frequently the custom amongst the masters of the trading vessels, in competing for the supplies of oil, to enhance the price for the mere purpose of opposing each other, which oftentimes brings it to as much as twenty coppers, without the least possible benefit accruing to any party but the natives, who are always ready to avail themselves of the differences which are productive of such advantage to them alone; for what one vessel pays the remainder must do the same or cease to trade, and oil purchased beyond fourteen or fifteen coppers, will on an average produce a loss to the merchant. Every article is estimated at so many copper rods, which constitute the currency of the country, and renders the trade intelligible to the most common understanding.

The traders of Egbosherry (which place is the principal oil market) only take copper rods in exchange, therefore the Callebar people are obliged to convert the goods they receive from the ships into copper rods at their own market previous to going thither; consequently in the event of a scarcity of rods (which frequently occurs) they experience infinite difficulty in obtaining the oil, although there may be a superfluity of it in the market. It would doubtless then be advisable to take a certain proportion of the cargo in rods, and allow two, three, or four on every ten crews; which would much facilitate the purchase. From the length of time since this article has been imported into the country, and the great avidity shewn to obtain them, you may get a copper and a half for each rod, particularly if new.

Duke Ephraim is the principal and most honorable trader of the place, he receives a third more than any one else for his oil, which difference is paid in salt, he is a good man, and it is of the utmost importance to keep on a friendly footing with him, for his influence amongst the tradesmen being absolute and so predominant, that in the event of dispute, he has it in his power to do much injury to your operations. It is even recommended to give him a better assortment of goods, and to humour him as far as circumstances will admit, but by no means to dissort your cargo, it being important to preserve a proportioned assortment of every article throughout the purchase. The importunities of the Duke, at the moment of payment are generally great, which renders it necessary (though indulgent) to be decided and not go beyond a certain point; it may be advised also to limit his credit (particularly in case of competition) to five hundred crews.

The great evil that ships are exposed to in this trade, is the necessity of giving credit, otherwise the natives have not wherewith to go to market for the oil; however to diminish this in some measure, the strictest inquiries ought to be made concerning those you deal with, taking care never to give more goods, than what you observe each individual is in the habit of accounting for the following market, otherwise they will run up a long debt, and then take their oil to another vessel.

The best and most indefatigable traders are the Creek Town people, to the king of which place (Eyo Honesty) it is necessary to observe the ceremony of a visit on arrival; for although he furnishes little or no oil, his patronage is nevertheless desirable, and it is customary to give him two more coppers than the rest for what oil he sells. Salt is a very profitable and commanding article here, therefore you cannot bring too much, for any superfluity may be disposed of to great advantage, at Camaroons. Fine India cloth is made use of in this trade, with the exception of some light colored Manchester handkerchief pieces, Glasgow Danes, and a few common romals to pay the comey with. The India cloths ought all to be well selected, with a great variety of pattern; for the versatility of taste amongst the Callebar people is very great. The Photas and the Phota romals being scarce, are highly prized, and recommended to be taken if attainable. Guns are much liked, but ought to be of good manufacture. Soap also is in great demand, and very profitable.

The measures in use are the crew and the powder keg, the former made to hold nine gallons and a half, which serves for oil, salt, and pepper, and the latter, a small keg to contain a little more than half a pint. The comey crew for salt is made only to contain 5 lbs.

The following is a list of the most suitable articles for the trade, with the price of each affixed.

Coppers.		Coppers.	
4	Salt per crew	2	Padlocks, common
4	Powder per keg	2	Metal Looking Glasses
8	Iron Bars, double	8 to 10	A Wedge of Soap
4	Ditto, single	1	Twenty Flints (which ought to be large)
2	India long Cloths, Romals, &c. per yard	10	Neat Rum per Gallon
1½	Manchester, ditto	8	Trade ditto
10	Red Taffeties, per yard	4	Large striped Worsted Caps
8	Bandanoes, per handkerchief	1	Small ditto
2	Photas and Chilloes, per yard	2	Scarlet ditto
3	Sastracundies, Antipos, Danes and Allijars, per yard		Beads assorted to their taste may be sold in Proportion as they are invoiced
3 to 4	Negro Hats		Ginghams
12 to 16	Fine ditto		A few Brass Pans
20	Leather ditto	10 to 14	Oil per Crew
50 to 60	Silver and gold laced ditto	3	Pepper ditto
2	Quart Mugs and Covers	1	Red Wood, per billet, weighing 60 to 80lbs.
½	Pint ditto	4 to 6	Ivory per lb.
36	Silk Umbrellas		Black Silk Handkerchiefs are a good Article and sell like the Bandanoes
4	Pewter Spoons, per dozen		
8	Iron ditto		
1	Knives		
24	Guns, Tower		
2 to 8	Bells, according to size		

A good supply of rum is necessary for this trade, for independent of the payment for the oil, it is customary to give a proportion to each trader, besides a small present (or dash) of cloth.

There are, upon an average, 72 lbs. of oil to the crew, and 56 of salt; running about thirteen crews to the puncheon, eleven to the hogshead, and nearly thirty-three to the ton.

The payments are made according to the following proportions, which with the above information, the merchant is rendered independent of the professed necessity of experience, and may make his calculations with the greatest accuracy, respecting both the outward and homeward cargo of a vessel of any tonnage.

A TABLE containing the various Terms of Payment for the Oil to be adapted in Proportion to the Competion that exists, and the Price that can be afforded at the time by the Merchant.

10 *Crews of Oil at* 8 *Cop.*		10 *Crews at* 10 *Coppers.*		10 *Crews at* 12 *Coppers.*	
10 Crews of Salt	40	10 Crews of Salt	40	10 Crews of Salt	40
2 Kegs of Powder··	8	2 Kegs of Powder..	8	2 Kegs of Powder ..	12
3 Iron Bars········	12	4 Iron Bars ······	16	4 Iron Bars	16
6 Yards of Romal..	12	1 Wedge of Soap..	8	1 Wedge of Soap ..	8
½ A wedge of Soap..	4	1 Looking Glass .	2	2 Quart Mugs······	4
1 Looking Glass, or ⎰	2	1 Quart Mug······	2	8 Yards of Romal..	16
6 Spoons .. ······⎱		1 Large striped Cap ⎰	4	2 Yds. of Sastracundi	6
1 Red Cap, or a ⎰	2	or 2 red Caps ..⎱		2 Large striped Caps	8
Quart Mug ....⎱		8 Yards of Romal ..	16	1 Red Cap	2
				1 Looking Glass....	2
	80		100	Beads ··········	2
					120

10 *Crews at* 10 *Coppers.*		10 *Crews at* 12 *Coppers*		10 *Crews at* 14 *Coppers*	
10 Crews of Salt	40	10 Crews of Salt	40	10 Crews of Salt····	40
2 Kegs of Powder..	8	2 Kegs of Powder ..	8	2 Kegs of Powder..	8
4 Iron Bars ······	16	4 Iron Bars ······	16	4 Iron Bars........	16
1 Piece of Romal ..	24	1 Piece of Romal ..	24	4 Copper Rods	4
2 Yards of Pocket ···	6	4 Yards of Pocket..	12	1 Piece of Romal ..	24
1 Large striped Cap	4	2 Large striped Caps	8	4 Yards of Pocket..	12
Other small Articles	2	1 Wedge of Soap .	8	2 Large striped Caps	8
		Small Articles for	4	1½ Wedge of Soap..	12
	100			Beads & other small ⎰	16
			120	Articles for ...⎱	
					140

One whole piece of Romal is here given to the 10 Crews, which, if it can be afforded, will secure custom, it being always preferable to small articles.

10 *Crews at* 12 *Coppers*		10 *Crews at* 14 *Coppers*		10 *Crews at* 16 *Coppers*	
10 Crews of Salt	40	10 Crews of Salt	40	10 Crews of Salt	40
4 Iron Bars ······	16	1 Piece of Romal ..	24	1½ Piece of Romal..	36
1 Piece of Romal..	24	4 Yards of Pocket..	12	4 Yards of Pocket ..	12
4 Yards of Pocket	12	3 Kegs of Powder..	12	4 Iron Bars ······	16
4 Copper Rods	4	4 Copper Rods ..	4	2 Wedges of Soap ..	16
1 Bandana Handker.	8	2 Bandanas	16	3 Kegs of Powder..	12
2 Kegs of Powder	8	4 Iron Bars ······	16	6 Copper Rods	6
Other Articles for	8	1½ Wedge of Soap..	12	1 Fine Hat	14
		Small Articles......	4	Small Articles for ..	8
	120		140		160

To the Duke who receives 4 more Coppers.

500 *Crews at* 14 *Coppers*		500 *Crews at* 16 *Coppers*		500 *Crews at* 18 *Coppers*	
1000 Crews of Salt ..	4000	1000 Crews of Salt ..	4000	1000 Crews of Salt ..	4000
1 Barrel of Powder	400	50 Romals········	1200	50 Romals	1200
10 Guns···········	240	130 Yards of Pocket	390	150 Yards of Pocket	450
8 Sastracundies ⎰	416	220 Iron Bars......	880	246 Iron Bars	960
16 Handker. ⎱		15 Wedges of Soap	120	20 Wedges of Soap	160
200 Iron Bars ······	800	200 Copper Rods·····	230	12 Guns ··········	288
2 Doz. large stri- ⎰	96	10 Guns ··········	240	300 Copper Rods ..	300
ped Caps....⎱		2 Doz. striped Caps	96	1 Barrel of Powder	400
2 Dozen red Caps	72	2 Doz. look. Glasses	48	2 Pieces of Bandana	112
40 Romals ······	960	1 Piece of Banda- ⎰	48	2 Doz. large stri- ⎰	96
Small Articles ..	16	na 7 Handker. ⎱		ped Caps ....⎱	
	7000	1 Barrel of Powder	400	2 Doz. look. Glasses	48
		The remainder in		An assortment of ⎰	980
		small Articles		other Articles ⎱	
			8000		900

It is advisable for those who intend remaining a season in this river, to have a house built over the vessel, by which means they protect the health of the crew, as well as the ship's decks and sides, which experience material damage, by being exposed to the powerful influence of the sun, during so great a length of time.

From Callebar to Cameroon's River.

From the East head, the land runs S.E. by S. a league and a half, as far as Backassy Gap, and from thence, E.N.E. 2¼ leagues, to a bluff point, called Backassy Point, which forms the West head of the entrance to Rio del Rey, off whence, there is a reef stretching out 2 miles to the Eastward, with a mud bank uniting with the East head, 2 miles off shore.

Two leagues and a half, North from Backassy Point, is a small river, called Qua Backassy ; from whence to Del Rey Point, on the same side, it is distant 1¼ league, beyond which 2 leagues, the river is navigable with a muddy bottom, and free channel in 3¼, 4, and 5 fathoms. Vessels bound to Callebar, should be careful in not overshooting their distance, and mistake this river for it, which, however by common observation, may be easily discriminated by the Backassy Gap, and the Rumby mountains on the East side of the river, abreast of Backassy Point, also the high land of Cameroon, 8 leagues to the Southward of the latter.*

Rumby greatly abounds in a very excellent species of ebony, which may be had for a mere trifle, as well as provisions of all sorts, hogs, goats, yams, &c.; but the natives are extremely treacherous, and ought to be strictly guarded against. From the high land of Cameroons, to three islands, called the Amboises off Bimbia, it is 5 leagues S.E. by S. ; the land is high and bluff about Bimbia

---

* The high land of Cameroons may be observed at an immense distance when clear, being of almost incredible height, and although nearly on the equator, is frequently capped with snow ; it seems to be little known in Geographical History, and only mentioned by an early Portuguese historian, who describes it as a volcano, which, however, neither the inhabitants of the country, or the neighbouring islands have the bhightest traditionary knowledge of.

Point, with a small river, called Rio Pequino, to the right, and only 4 and 5 fathoms all along shore, with a muddy bottom, to a head land, called the False Cape, with some tall trees on it; it is then 4½ leagues; the land very low and flat, the true Cape Cameroons being nearly 2 miles round the Point to the Eastward, and lies in 3° 37' North latitude, and 9° 20' East longitude, with a spit of sand half a league to the Southward, and another called the Middle Bank, 5 miles E.S.E. from the Cape, to clear which, bring the Cape to bear North, and Malimba Point East, then steer for the latter, until you open Sandy Island to the Westward of Bluff Island, and the rugged trees on Gallows Point bear N.E. ½ E. which you may run for over the flats; you are clear of the flats when in 3½ fathoms, within half a mile of the East side of the rugged trees, and will be then abreast the three banks, called the middle ground, to avoid which, keep along the North shore, in 5 fathoms, about a mile out, as far as the bushes; and then to the anchorage opposite King George's Town, in 5 fathoms, keeping Doctor's Point well open to starboard, on account of a shoal that runs out 1½ mile; there is a rise of 8 feet at spring tides, when it flows at 6. The South side of the Cameroon's entrance is formed by Bluff Island, 6 miles N.W of which is a chain of heavy breakers, called the Dogs' Heads, and 3 miles N. by W. a small sandy island with a few bushes on it. The Dogs' Heads break violently, and may be seen at a long distance; if passing them running to the Southward with a flood-tide, give them a good birth, for the flood sets rapidly over them.

On the Cameroon's Trade.

The principal produce of this river is ivory and palm oil; and un-til very recently, vessels have only resorted hither for the former, which has always been particularly abundant, and of a very su-perior quality, but of late it has become equally celebrated for its supplies of oil, which the natives discovering to be much in demand, begin to collect very largely; and there is not the least doubt but that it will in a very few years even surpass Callebar, from the cir-cumstance of the greater prevalence of the palm-tree in the imme-

diate neighbourhood, and is to be had at a much lower rate.   The
ivory is generally speaking very large, as well as of excellent
species, and so inexhaustible is the supply here, that sixty tons are
known to have been procured in one season, by English vessels and
Portuguese from the islands.   The mode of procuring it is very peculiar, differing from that of any part of the coast, it being all taken
from the dead elephant, in the following manner :   About 200 miles
inland, S.E. from Cameroons, there is an immense tract of desart,
with a contiguous morass, where the elephants come in droves to
quench their thirst, and where in the avid pursuit of water, they get
immersed in the marsh from whence being unable to extricate themselves, they die ; many again are found dead in the desart where
they expire from extreme exhaustion.   The natives describe the
stench, arising from putrefaction, to be quite poisonous, and never
attempt to approach the place under the influence of the sun, consequently, make all their excursions thither by night, which is even
then not unfrequently attended with death.

There are three large towns called Mungo, Batimba, and Be-
limba, to which the ivory is all carried, having communicating paths
with the morasses, and are the principal depôts from whence
Cameroons is supplied.

The system of barter here is the bar trade, consequently, every
article is valued at so many iron bars; it is better, however, not at
all times to be guided by this mode, but to give an assortment of
goods according to the nature of the tooth, and to the extent you
can afford.

The following list contains the most suitable articles for this market.

Manchester Romals of various patterns	Flints
A few Shawls and fancy ditto	Brass Pans
Blue Bafts	Neptunes
White Bafts	Bone hafted Knives, pointed
Nicanees	Earthen Ware, Mugs, Jugs and Salt
Chilloes	Fine Hats, and a few laced
Guns, strong Tower	Small Deal Trade Boxes
Bandanas	Metal Looking Glasses
A few striped Silks	Large sized ones of different dimensions
Iron Bars	and patterns, which are a favorite
Powder	article
Bells assorted	A few other small Things may be added
Padlocks	such as Glass Ware, Caps, Spoons and
Umbrellas, a few large ones	Beads
Copper Rods	Rum

Salt is the most essential ingredient in this river, it very much reduces the cost of the cargo; also, being in such great demand, you will scarcely be able to trade without it, in case of competition; a pork-barrel with the top cut off has generally been the measure for it; but a crew made of about twelve gallons may be substituted. In making an assortment for a very fine tooth allow one neptune, which article is greatly prized. The guns must be very good for this river, and high proof; trade boxes with a small padlock and key are invariable in requisition; numbers of which may be made on the outward passage by the ship's carpenter, at a very trifling expense : Soldiers' jackets are liked by the natives, and old rich court dresses by the chiefs.

The oil of Cameroons, like that of Benin is of a very superior nature, being all boiled, and not obtained by compression as that of Callebar; it is sold at from two to four bars (according to competition) per crew of twelve gallons, which is paid for in a regular assortment of goods.

The river is governed by two chiefs, King Bell and King Acqua, residing on opposite sides, whose interest it is necessary to court, they are great holders of ivory, and are desirous of supporting a trade with the English, who they respect in preference to any other nation.

A Description of the Islands in the Bight of Biaffra namely Fernandepo, Princes, St. Thomas, and Anno Bom.

In this bight two currents meet within the vicinity of Fernandepo, the one from the Westward along the Coast of Guinea, and the other from the Southward from the Coast of Angola, which is generally speaking the most powerful; on account of which merchant vessels bound from Callebar or Cameroons, to Princes or St. Thomas are in the habit of beating up along shore, as far as Cape St. John's, and Gabon striking off from thence for their point of destination, from the very erroneous idea that the current in shore is less rapid, and that thereby they secure a quicker passage, whereas reason and experience teach us that the velocity of a stream is considerably increased at those points where it meets with resistance, which cause we may assign for the great vigour of its progress in the immediate vicinity of the islands.

It is therefore urged as most advisable, to beat in a direct line between the islands, choosing if convenient, the full or change of the moon, at which periods the current is frequently known to run strong to windward. Observe also, when the wind is fresh the current is generally strongest to leeward, but with calm weather and light breezes is oftentimes weatherly.

FERNANDEPO is a large island, due South from Callebar river, lying N.E. and S.W. about 40 miles in length; its North point being in 3° 40′ North latitude, and 8° 40′ East longitude; it was formerly occupied by the Portuguese, who erected a fort on the East side; then given up to the Spaniards, who were driven out for their extreme cruelty and ill treatment, by the natives who now live in a perfect savage state of nature; it is most luxuriantly fertile, and may be said to equal any of our West India islands, it spontaneously produces an abundance of fruits and vegetables of all sorts, particularly yams which may be obtained for a mere trifle; only it is necessary to guard against treachery, for the predatory acts of many contraband slave vessels have rendered them inexpressibly revengeful. The land is remarkably high, and may be seen from 25 to 26 leagues off; when to the Westward it appears in three conic mountains, tapering away towards the South end which lies in 3° 5′ North.

Sailing between this island and Cameroons, do not approach too near the East side, where you are liable to get becalmed. Nothing can be more decidedly advantageous or better calculated for the establishment of a settlement than this island, lying at a small distance from the coast, it is freely ventilated by the sea breezes, and from its eligible position commands the trade of four navigable rivers, namely, Benin, Bonny, Callebar, and Cameroons, whose commercial pursuits are rapidly increasing, and which being annually more frequented, present very flattering prospects of becoming very shortly a medium, through which, civilization and christianity may be successfully disseminated in the interior. The island possesses two convenient roadsteads, one on the East side abreast the old fort, and the other on the N.W. side, to the Westward of Goat Island, called the N.W. Bay, both of which are supplied with fresh water.

PRINCES is a small island S.W. from Fenandepo in the possession of the Portuguese, and the residence of a governor ; it is of supermarine volcanic production, covered with a variety of elevated and pointed mountains, which at a distance of 10 or 12 leagues appear like detached islands, particularly the Parrot's Bill, which is a round topped hill in the form of a sugar loaf : there is a good harbour and bay, at the bottom of which is a town defended by several batteries, the first of which is a small white one, on a hill to the left on entering, the principal fort on the same side round the point; and another on the summit of the right entrance of the bay.

On the S.E. side of the island there is a high round rock, or islet, with white chalky cliffs, called the Dutchman's Cap, between which and the main, there is water for the largest vessels to pass.

Four leagues to the Westward of the Dutchman's Cap, are three rocks, called the Three Brothers ; do not come too near them with the lee current, which sets strong over them.

About $3\frac{1}{2}$ leagues from the Dutchman's Cap, on the East side, there is a small sandy bay, with good anchorage in 10 and 12 fathoms, and a good bottom, coming whence give a birth to the South Point, where there is a small rocky ledge ; having passed the North point of the bay, where there is a small sunken rock, you descry the white battery on the summit of another point, when round, which the town appears, and then the large fort on the larboard side, abreast of whence is a rock a quarter of a mile out, visible only at low water, called the Fort Rock; independent of this there is no danger in the harbour but what is seen, and the anchorage is extremely safe and well sheltered from all the prevalent winds, except the tornadoes, which blow directly in, and require to be provided against during their season.

There are from 6 to 9 fathoms at the entrance of the bay, but the best anchorage is abreast the fort in 4 and 5 fathoms, amid channel, from whence you have easy access to the town, and a good watering place to the right of the fort, with abundant supplies from a rocky spring.

On arrival here it is necessary to report the vessel to the governor, who sends custom-house officers on board, at the ship's expense, which amounts to a quarter dollar per diem. And on quitting the harbour forty dollars are exacted for port dues and anchorage, in addition to which, if you profess to come for trade, the customs demand forty more.

The winds, in the vicinity of these islands, are generally between the South and West, with a land wind out of the harbour in the morning; therefore, in sailing out of Princes, endeavour to get under weigh with this breeze, keeping well over to the South shore, for as you advance outside, the wind gradually draws to the Southward, which with the swell sets you to the North side, where there is a large rock called the Diamond Rock, above water, N.W. of which is Goat Island, forming the Northern extremity of Princes.

If the current is running to the N.E. when you approach this island, make it on the South side, or you will be swept to leeward and prevented fetching the harbour, but if to the S.W. make it on the North side.

There is rarely a clear atmosphere about the land, but when clear the island may be seen at a distance of 14 or 15 leagues, and from its mountains are distinguished the Peak of Fernandepo. In case of thick weather your approach to the island is indicated and known by an incredible quantity of gulls, hovering to and fro in its direction. The harbour lies in 1° 38′ North latitude, and 7° 10′ East longitude, by good observations of the author in 1816.

If homeward bound and the wind far Southerly, do not (as is generally considered) think it necessary to beat to the Southward of St. Thomas before you stand to the Westward, but if to windward of Princes, and the wind admits of your making Westing without Northing, keep on the larboard tack, and you will find not only the current diminish but the wind (though lighter) gradually veering to the Southward, so as to enable you to cross into the trades.

St. Thomas lies about 24 leagues S.S.W. of Princes, it is 12 leagues in length and 7 in breadth, with an undulated succession of

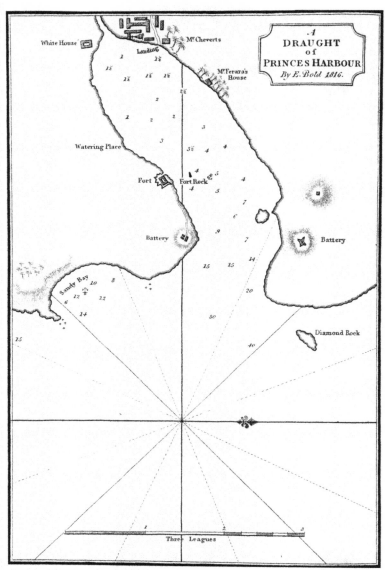

DRAUGHT of PRINCES HARBOUR
By E. Bold 1816.

White House

Mr. Cheverts

Landing

Mr. Ferara's House

Watering Place

Fort   Fort Rock

Battery

Sandy Bay

Battery

Diamond Rock

Three Leagues

Engraved by W.G.Rowe.

Princes bearing N.N.W. 12 Leagues

Princes bearing N.W.b.N. 5 Leagues

A. Parrots Bill

high mountains, terminating in a peak which is 8000 feet from the level of the sea, with a gap near the summit, declining to a low point of land to the South, where there is a small islet, called Rolle's Island, which is situated on the equator in 6° 35′ East longitude, with 22° 15′ Westerly variation. Between this island and the main is a commodious and excellent harbour, being the best and most sheltered of all the African islands, having safe anchorage for the largest vessels; in coming whence avoid the Seven Stones, which are the only danger, and are several high rocks lying 6 miles E.N.E. from Rolle's Island. From thence to the islet of St. Anna, or the Postillion's Cap, it is a bold and clear shore with several small villages on the coast, and the town of St. Anna opposite the islet, from whence to the town and fort of Anna de Chaves it is 2½ leagues. The town lies at the bottom of the bay, with a fort on the South point, and Cabrita Island W. by N. of the North point, in 30′ North latitude. The best anchorage in the roads is in 4 or 5 fathoms, sandy bottom, the fort bearing W. by S. and Cabrita Island N. by E. ½ E.

Vessels pay the same dues here as at Princes, but it is a place of infinitely less trade, it produces however a greater abundance of fruits and stock of all sorts, which are to be had at a very moderate rate. Traders are cautioned not to take any gold at these islands without proving it with aquafortis, it being most commonly adulterated with yellow sand and brass filings. The body of St. Thomas lies about 40 leagues West from the river Gabon; on the South side of the island is a remarkable hill in the form of a church-steeple, and two or three good watering places on the East coast.

Anno Bom is a small healthy island, about 8 leagues in circumference, lying S.W. by S. from St. Thomas, in latitude 1° 30′ South, and 5° 30′ East longitude, it is high mountainous land, covered with orange and lime trees, with a beautiful fresh water-pond on the summit; it is only inhabited by blacks, who for any sort of old clothing and salt, which they much appreciate, will most liberally exchange hogs, goats, cows, deer, poultry, and fruits, with which the island abounds. There is anchorage on the N.E. side, between the village and a small island, in 10 and 12 fathoms, good sandy bottom, but vessels never frequent this place excepting for provisions, which may be procured by lying to, a few hours near the village. There is a small island off the East point, with a clear passage between, also several rocks close in shore on the South, but no danger that is not visible.

Description of the Coast from Cameroons to Cape St. John, and from thence to Cape Lopez, including the Rivers Gabon and Danger.

From Buff Island the land runs very low, S.E. by S. 10 leagues, and from thence 2½ leagues S.W. forming the bight of Pannavia, in which there is only 5 to 7 fathoms, 3 leagues from the shore.

From Point Garajam (which is the South end of the bight) the land is hilly, but declines to very low flat country, continuing in a S.S.W. direction, as far as the river Campo, 32 leagues; this river is small and only navigable for boats, having breakers on the starboard, entrance with 16 fathoms abreast the mouth; it may be known by two hills seen to the Northward of it, called the Saddle, from the gap at the summit; the other the Table Hill, on account of its flat level top.

Thirteen miles from Campo there is a small village, called Bata, close to the shore, with good anchorage in 6 fathoms, half a league out. From hence you see a chain of inland mountains, called the Seven Hills, but nothing to render them remarkable, excepting the centre one, being the highest. To Heybern Head or the river St. Benito, it is then 10 leagues, S.W. by S. a very low thickly wooded coast; the Head is easily known by its remarkably bluff point, on which there is a hill; the entrance of the river is narrow, with only 3 fathoms, and separates into two branches, 4 or 5 miles up to the E.N.E. and E.S.E. up which a very extensive trade for ivory was formerly carried on by the Portuguese. The South point is rocky, from a little within the river to some distance down the coast, but is steep to half a league from it.

From Heybern Head to Cape St. John's it is 10 leagues, S. by W. ½ W. with a double hill, inland, called the Mitre, from which the coast forms a sort of bight to St. John's ; it is bold and rocky, without any beach.   Cape St. John's is very bluff, and may be seen a considerable distance, without any land appearing to the Southward when North of it; it is surrounded by a reef of rocks, and forms the North side of the Rio D'Angra, which is now corrupted and better known by the name of the river Danger; it lies in 1° 16′ North latitude, and 8° 40′ East longitude.   S. by E. from the Cape lies Corisco, a long low island, 4 leagues in length and 2 broad, with a sand bank along the West side, about a league out, and on the North two small banks lying East and West, nearly a league from the land.   Five miles East of the great island is Little Corisco, but inaccessible on account of a ledge of rocks, reaching from thence to Mosquito Island to the N.W. which stands at the narrow entrance of the river, and has a bar of sand connected with it from the opposite shore, with only 2½ and 3 fathoms on it, but deep water on each side, from 5 to 7 fathoms.

When the Cape bears North about 2½ miles, steer E.S.E. towards Mosquito Island, taking care to avoid the Corisco banks; when abreast of that island steer E. by N. over the bar, as far as the town of Angra, nearly 3½ leagues up on the larboard side, where you may anchor in 5 or 6 fathoms, sand and gravel ; it is navigable 3 or 4 leagues farther up in the same direction, and contracts into a very narrow channel taking a N.E. course.

Two and a half leagues South from the South point of Corisco island, is Cape Esteiras, (the South side of the river Danger) between whence is a bank of breakers, amid-channel, with a passage of 3 or 4 fathoms on each side, leading to the river between the two islands of Corisco; from the said breakers steer N.E. in the direction of the little island, until the Easternmost side of the great island bears N.N.W. to clear the bank, which lies 3 miles East of the South point ; then steer for the North side, bordering on its shore, to avoid the bank which extends 3 miles from the small island ; when you get the river open, run for the bar keeping Mosquito Island a little open on the starboard bow, and when on the bar, as before directed.   The tide flows here at 5½ᴴ with the full and change.

The river is much frequented by the Portuguese from the adjacent islands, and produces a quantity of ivory, ebony, bar-wood, and pod pepper, which may be obtained at a very moderate rate, for common cloths, iron ware, tobacco, rum, beads, &c. By coming to an anchor off Corisco you may load your ship with barwood in a very few days. But to procure ivory which is in great abundance, it is necessary to trade up the river as far as Angra, and from the extreme treachery of the natives you are obliged to be armed, during all your transactions with them.

From Cape Esteiras, the land trenches away to the S.E. forming what is called the Bight of Esteiras, where there is anchorage in 6 or 7 fathoms, sandy bottom ; from thence the coast runs South, thickly wooded as far as Cape Clara, which from the former Cape is 8 leagues ; it is a high bluff point, and with Round Corner (which is 5 leagues to the southward) forms the entrance into Gabon river, at whose centre lie two shoals N.N.W. and S.S.E. from each other, with a channel of 3 fathoms between their northernmost point, and Cape Clara, which is distant five miles.

From Round Corner (which is known by its peak, and has a bank half a league to the Westward) the land runs three leagues N.E. to a low flat sandy shore, called Sandy Point.

Three leagues within the river, from Cape Clara, there are two islands, King's or Prince's Island on the North shore, and Parrot Island on the South ; between which is a clear passage, with 6 or 7 fathoms, from hence the river branches off to the N.E. and S.E. the former of which is the main, or Gabon River, and is the principal trading place, with a town called King Glass's Town, 3½ leagues from King's Island on the larboard shore.

From Cape St. John's to Gabon, the soundings are regular, with muddy bottom ; and in 20 fathoms you are 5 leagues from the shore.

Sailing into Gabon bring Cape Clara to bear N.E. about three miles, when you will be within the bank, then steer S.E. for the middle of the river, until Prince's Island bears E. by S. running between it and Parrot Island ; when to the Eastward of them, keep away for the North shore to avoid the bank that runs five miles West of Gabon Point, which you are clear of when the North end of

Prince's bears West; then run along shore as far as King Glass's Town, which is the great trading mart.

Coming from the Southward into Gabon River you may enter between the South Bank and Sandy Point, taking care to give the latter a birth of two miles, there being a foul bank reaching all the way from Rough Corner, with not more than two fathoms at high water; and from Sandy Point to the South end of Parrot Island, there is a bank stretching from the South shore, along whence the ebb runs with great violence and rippling to the S.W.

It is high water on the full and change at six, rising **7** to 8 feet. Cape Clara lies in 25′ North latitude, and 8° 35′ East longitude, with 23° Westerly variation.

It must be observed, the winds all along this coast, from June to October, vary very much from the S.S.W. to S.S.E. in the twenty-four hours, which renders it advisable for vessels beating to the Southward, to tack accordingly, and take every advantage of a slant, also to stand in for the shore after midnight, for the benefit of the land wind, which sets in towards the early part of the morning. The current most commonly runs here about 18 miles in the twenty-four hours, to the Northward, varying sometimes with the change of the moon, to the Southward.

From Round Corner, the land runs S. by E. 10 leagues, to a small island, called Fanaes close to the main, with a white down interspersed with trees; it is then 1½ league to the river Nazareth, which may be distinguished by a remarkable clump of trees on the South side, where the entrance is bordered by a sandy flat, running out 3 leagues due West, between which and the above-mentioned island forms a sort of bay, with good anchorage in 3 and 4 fathoms. The coast from thence continues in a similar direction, 14 leagues to Montong town and river, a low sandy shore, and a continuance of the former bank, 2½ leagues out, with a small island half-way. From Montong the coast runs S.W. to Cape Lopez river, and thence to Cape Lopez, N.E. 7 leagues, forming an extensive bay, with a good sheltered roadstead, in 4, 6, and 8 fathoms, off Fettish Point, in approaching whence take care of the French bank, the South point of which, lies 2½ leagues N.E. by E. from the Cape, and

o

extends the same distance towards the opposite shore, with only 2 fathoms on it, but a clear channel on each side into the bay. From Gabon to Cape Lopez, which lies in the same longitude, the course is due South, 24 leagues; the Cape is very low, but bold round both sides within half a mile, appearing at a short distance rugged, with bushes close to the water. In coasting down to Cape Lopez, do not come nearer the bank on the main than 8 or 10 fathoms. The Cape lies in 1° 9′ South latitude. This place is very little frequented by others than the Portuguese from the islands, who procure considerable quantities of ivory in exchange for common cloths, particularly the Jaboo, with bafts, guns, powder, tobacco, &c. The town of Libatta, 6 leagues from Fettish Point, is extensive, and the residence of a king, who frequently furnishes abundant supplies of teeth. Provisions are scarce here and the water not good.

A Description of the Coast from Cape Lopez to the Congo.

The whole of this Coast, according to the charts and instructions, is laid down very inaccurately, being as much too far to the Westward, as the windward coast and Guinea are to the Eastward. You may run from Cape Lopez to the Congo in 16 fathoms, all the way without danger, when you will, generally speaking, be about 3 leagues from the land, with ooze or sandy bottom. The winds during the fine weather are from the S.W. which set in after noon, with land breezes from the N.E. early in the morning, but during the rains and winter months the winds are from the Southward, with little or no land breeze. The current runs with great rapidity in the vicinity of the land, therefore vessels bound to any particular part of this coast should not think of approaching the land, until on the parallel of their destination, unless the current should be found weatherly.

Six leagues from Cape Lopez, there is a bight or bay, with two small rivers, one on the North side, and the other on the South, and 3 leagues farther, a more extensive bay and river, called Mexias, which is rendered inaccessible, by a bank of sand at the mouth, abreast of which, however, there is good anchorage on the North side, in 5 and 6 fathoms, but take care to avoid the South shore, from whence the rocks run nearly half-way across; the coast from hence is all bold and safe, and may be approached within 6 and 8 fathoms.

From the South Point to the False Cape it is 5½ leagues, S.S.E. a low woody coast, with the two intervening rivers, Fernan Vaz, and then 5 leagues S. by E. to Cape St. Catherine, on the North side of which is a considerable bight, named Camma, at the mouth of a river of the same name; the Cape is in 9° 35' East longitude, and known by a tuft of trees, which in coming from the North-ward appears separated from the land, with a rough craggy shore on the West; from the Cape there is a ledge of rocks and sand, stretching out about a league to the N.W. with good anchorage in 6 and 8 fathoms inside, and a sandy bottom.

From Cape St. Catherine the coast runs 5 leagues to the S.E. to a very low point and small island; and from thence to River Setté, 5 leagues S.E. by E. with a very flat coast covered with trees, which may be seen if clear in 29 fathoms. The River Setté forms the Northern limits of the Loango dominions, and about 20 leagues up, has a large town of the same name, which formerly used to carry on an extensive trade with the Portuguese, on the coast and the countries inland, which produce an abundance of the finest species of bar-wood and ivory; the land on each side the entrance of the river is excessively low, and covered with high trees, which render it indiscernable until very close: there is a bar across the mouth, with only 3 fathoms outside and 2 inside, but good anchorage in 6 fathoms, the North entrance of the river bearing N.E. From Setté to Point Pedras the coast runs 10 leagues S.S.E. a low flat shore, but high mountains to be seen inland, called The Hills of the Holy Ghost, covered with the most beautiful clumps of trees down the mountains; the two centre ones of which appear high, but flat at the summit, declining with a gentle declivity to the North and South; the ground is all extremely foul along this coast, which you ought not to approach nearer than 7 or 8 fathoms. Off Point Pedras there is a stony reef reaching half a league to seaward, which give a good birth to in rounding.

From the Point to Cape Mayumba it is 7½ leagues S.E. by S. an uneven coast, with an undulating line of hills about half way, extending with a gradual rise to the pitch of the Cape, which forms a sort of hummock, and is the highest point, being steep down to the sea, with clumps of trees on the summit; it lies in 3° 35′ South latitude, and 11° 15′ East longitude, the needle varying two points to the Westward. From the pitch a rocky ledge runs out half a league to the S.W. the coast from thence falling back to the Eastward, forming with Point Matooti, the Bay of Mayumba, or the Bay of Alvaro of the Portuguese.

To the South of Mayumba, also, the land rises with three or four gradual elevations, covered with trees, and may be recognized by its sandy beach with several patches on the hills.

The bay is extremely commodious for anchoring, being quite clear, with a fine sandy bottom all round, in from 4 to 7 fathoms, excepting off Point Matooti, where a reef of rocks runs half a league to the N. ¼ E. many of which are above water and occasionally break with great violence; there are also some rocks about a mile and a half to the Eastward, within which is the common place for anchorage, in 6 or 7 fathoms abreast the factories, where it is well sheltered by the reef. To the Eastward of these factories there is an inlet to an inner bay, over which is a bar navigable only for small craft, having but 1 and 1½ fathoms over. From Cape Matooti the coast runs about 10 leagues to a low point, called Banda Point, where the ground is all foul with rocks and coral; from hence to Kilongo River the course is S.E. ¼ E. 6 leagues, moderately high land with white patches, and several intervening inlets or creeks. The South point of the river is a low cape, off which there is a reef to seaward, nearly a mile in length, with a convenient little cove to the Southward in 5 fathoms.

The Town of Kilongo is about 1½ league up the river, with a beautiful surrounding country, having an ornamental parkish appearance from the sea.

From Kilongo, the same course 6¼ leagues will bring you opposite the River Quiloo, which may be known by two remarkable bushes close together on the North side of the entrance.

From Quiloo, the land trenches away to the E.S.E. 4 leagues as far as the bottom of Loango Bay, which is known by its red clay hills on the North side, of moderate elevation, tufted with clumps of palm trees, and marked with ravines, or fissures; they resem- ble dirty chalk cliffs, and gradually decline to a low land, in the centre of the bay, from whence the coast takes a S.W. direction 2 leagues, as far as Indian Point, a long cape of land similar to the Bill of Portland, with a reef of breakers stretching 1 league to the Westward, and must not be approached too near; the point lies in 4° 37ʹ South latitude, and 12° 20ʹ East longitude. The an- chorage within the bay is in 4 or 6 fathoms, a large tuft of trees named Looboo Wood bearing S.E. Three miles inland are several large trading towns, the capital of which is Boali, or Loango, with an extensive royal palace in the centre: the inhabitants are perfectly black, with mild agreeable manners; and the Portuguese resort here for ivory with which it greatly abounds. The current runs with velocity along this coast at the rate of a mile and a half per hour.

Three leagues S.S.E. from Indian Point is a very low rocky cape called Black Point, three miles N.W. from whence runs a ledge with a deep bay inside, and a commodious sheltered roadstead, in 4 to 7 fathoms. From hence to Louiza Louanga River, the coast runs S. by E. 6 leagues, a low white sandy beach, with elevated land on the right of the river, from a point called South Point; 2 leagues farther South is the River Kagongo, which is 2 leagues in breadth, with a line of red hills on the starboard shore, steep down to the strand, at which extremity is Malemba Bay, open to the sea, but good anchorage in 5 or 6 fathoms, within 2 miles of the shore.

From Malemba Point the coast runs S.E. 4 leagues, to a small river called Belè, being the Northern limit of the Kingdom of Angoy, also of Cabenda Bay, which may be considered the most conveni- ent on this part of the coast, formed on the South by a tongue of land called Point Palmar, or Cabenda Hook; it has a reef of rocks on its North side, which give a good birth to when sailing into the bay, where you anchor in 5 fathoms, a large spreading tree on the South bearing S.E. by S. 2 miles, and the point W.S.W. taking care to avoid the banks off the River Belè.

Two and a half leagues S.S.E. from Point Palmar is Red Point, which is easily known by two intervening hills; a league from the point, a reef of rocks lies North and South, from whence to Point Palmeirinho, (which forms the North side of the Congo entrance) it is S.E. by S. 6 leagues, then 6 more to Fathomless Point, where the river contracts to a breadth of only 2½ miles.

Description of the Congo.

The Congo (or Zahir of the natives) is one of the most navigable and magnificent rivers of West Africa, it is accessible for large vessels up to the falls of Gamba Enzaddi, which lie at the Eastern extremity of the Congo dominions, being upwards of 80 leagues, in an E. by N. direction from the entrance, and from whence, on account of an immense chain of the Coanza and Acquilonda mountains, the river stretches Northward, which (according to the ocular demonstration, and positive assurances of an intelligent black Portuguese, whom the author conversed with) continues in a similar line for a considerable distance; hence we may justly infer the probability of its proving a continuation of the Niger, which idea is still farther supported by the circumstance of the Congo's swelling during the dry season of September, at which period, all the rivers North of the line are overflowing.

The seasons are considerably later here than to the Northward. Massanza, or the rains commence in October and terminate in January, when Neasu, or the harvest months succeed, continuing until March or April. Quitombo, or the tornado season takes place in May and June, followed by Quibiso, the dry season, until September, when the river experiences a considerable rise.

The winds from September to March are most commonly between the South and West, with a rapid current to the North, but from

March to the dry season, from the S.S.E. at which period the current frequently runs to the S.W. The sea breeze generally sets in towards noon ; and it may be observed, vessels bound along this coast to the Southward, should invariably beat to seaward out of the strength of the current, excepting when it should be found weatherly, and at those hours the land winds prevail, which they may stand in shore to take advantage of.

The velocity of the Congo's stream is great, but very unequal to the exaggerated accounts of many navigators ; although with light winds, and sometimes for the want of skill and judgment a vessel may be prevented entering for days.

The West Point of the mouth lies in 6° 15′ South latitude, and 12° 34′ East longitude, its greatest width at the entrance being 2 leagues, between Cape Padron and Point Palmeirinho, which contracts to two miles and a half, abreast of Fathomless Point, to whence from the latter, there is a bank called the Mona Maza, with regular soundings from the land, which must not be approached nearer than 5 fathoms. Over this bank the stream runs with excessive rapidity, the water retaining its sweetness full 8 or 10 miles N.W. of the river, and producing visible effects, with a black cast at a distance of 30 or 40 miles, where considerable quantities of green-wood and masses of roots are met with, particularly during the overflowings of the river.

From Cape Padron the land runs about a league and a half round Turtle Corner, to a point called Shark Point, (known by its thickly wooded hillocks) where there is a most celebrated fishing bank in 5 to 15 fathoms, and immediately off the bank upwards of a hundred ; round the point the land trenches away to the S.W. forming Deigos, or Sonhios Bay, which is interspersed with shoals. From this bay the current sets directly to the North, towards Mona Maza, at the rate of 6 miles per hour; therefore, vessels sailing into this river, should endeavour to enter with the sea breeze, keeping close to the land from Turtle Corner to Shark Point, crossing Deigos Bay in 6 or 7 fathoms, and from thence along the South shore in 4 and 5 fathoms, past Banza River to Knoxes Island, distant 7 or 8 leagues; from thence the water deepens to Oyster Haven, which is 4 leagues up on the same side abreast of Loo Cala Town. From the Haven a bank of only 1½ and 2 fathoms runs three miles to the Eastward, which you must avoid by keeping in 12 fathoms, and steering for a small island amid channel, called Hope's Island; from thence the river branches off to the N.E. and S.E. the latter of which is the safest channel; therefore, from Hope's Island, when in 9 fathoms, steer for Tonyanga Point, keeping the South shore close on board all the way up until you come to Sea Cow Bank, where you must cross over to Robson's Creek and Island, and from thence to the West end of Anglesey Island, where there is good anchorage and a considerable place for trade. The current varies in velocity all the way up the river, encreasing where it is interrupted by windings or islands.

The use of chain cables, for mooring, are particularly recommended in these waters, which are excessively destructive to hemp.

This river by the present mercantile world appears to be totally forgotten and neglected, notwithstanding its many advantages and the inducements its produce holds forth to adventurers, who would give encouragement to its trade; for independent of the incredible quantity of elephants' teeth it could furnish if demanded, it abounds in palm oil sufficiently to supply annually numerous vessels; but at present, that article (on account of the total explosion of traffic with Europeans) is not collected, and the nuts left to decay and waste their valuable juices on the earth. The natives are civil and accommodating, and extremely desirous of traffic : All sorts of common Manchester cloths, iron bars, ware, looking-glasses, guns, powder, and beads are best adapted, together with copper and brass utensils. The principal trading place and most inhabited part of the river is on the borders of the kingdom of Embomma, between Fingal's Shield, and a considerable town called Banza Embomma.

A Description of the Coast from Cape Padron to Loando St. Paul.

From Cape Padron the coast takes a S.W. by S. direction about 6 leagues as far as Cape Deceit, a bold shore with red cliffs all along, then 3 leagues South to Margate Bluff, from whence it is high land as far as Cape Funta and Bay, which is 8 leagues S. ½ E. having a shoal running 1 league to the Southward of the Cape, with anchorage inside the bay in 6 fathoms.

From hence Palmar Point on the North side of Ambriz Bay it is 17 leagues S.S.E. with the River Cousa intervening, known by its clump of high trees on the North side.

AMBRIZ BAY is nearly 3 leagues deep at the mouth of the river of the same name, formed by Point Palmar, (which is low) to the North, and Strong Tide Corner, or Cape Ambriz on the South; both of which are bordered with rocky ledges, over whence the sea breaks with impetuous force; the best anchorage is the entrance of the river (which is known by a high cliffy hill) bearing S.E. by E. in 5 fathoms muddy ground. The River Doce on the North side of Point Palmar must not be mistaken for Ambriz River; it may be distinguished by a hill inland called Mount Aravat.

CAPE AMBRIZ lies in 8° 2′ South latitude, and 13° 10′ East longitude, with 24 degrees Westerly variation; from whence to Great Mazula Roads and River, it is 9 leagues S.E. known by a cluster of round hills on the North, called the Seven Hills, and the Mazula Hills on the South stretching as far as the River Dandè, 5 leagues S.E. and forms the Northern boundary of the kingdom of Angola, it is navigable for vessels of 12 feet draught, some distance past a large town of the same name, where the Portuguese have a settlement, and carry on an extensive trade from the Brazils and their islands on the coast. The south entrance, called Dandè Point, is high barren land, with steep cliffs near the shore, variegated with red and white patches; from whence the coast runs S. S. E. 3½ leagues to Bengo River and Bay, which is formed by Lobster's Hummock, 2½ leagues S.W. by S. and Loando Island. Sailing into the bay bring the hummock to bear S.S.W. to clear the shoal off Loando Island. Three miles from Lobster's Hummock is the town of Loando St. Paul, which is a Portuguese settlement and the capital of Angola, it is the most civilized and splendid European settlement on the West Coast of Africa, being large and comparatively hand-some, containing several Roman Catholic churches and convents, with 7,000 inhabitants, one-third of which are whites; the houses are principally constructed of stone covered with tiles, and the place defended by a handsome fort ; its port or bay is well-sheltered and commodious for the largest vessels, with 8 to 10 fathoms in the centre. Two miles to the West of the Hummock is St. Peter's Island, on which stands the ruins of a fort ; you may sail between it and the great island, which you must keep close on board, and from whence you steer for the anchorage at the North end of the town, in 3½ and 4 fathoms, taking care to avoid the bank abreast it, which dries at low water, but has a passage of 70 yards in breadth between it and the town.

Loando, or the Great Island extends about 6 leagues from the N.E. to the S.W. and 2 miles in breadth, containing seven or eight villages, and produces an abundance of fruits ; there is a shoal of 2 fathoms, stretching 3½ miles N.E. from the North end, with a bar of 4 fathoms across the Curimba entrance, at the South point, which is defended by Fort St. Fernào.

The trade of this place is carried on with great vigour, principally by the Portuguese from the islands and the Brazilians, who carry away cassia, furs, and considerable quantities of ivory, which they export to Europe to great advantage.   The natives are mild, tractable, and easy to deal with ; they receive in exchange for their produce, copper and brass utensils, beads, Manchester cloths, iron bars, carpets, silks and other small articles, with guns and powder. It is to be wondered at, that the whole of this coast should be so little resorted to by the English, who have it in their power to furnish such superior merchandize, and might thereby carry on a trade extremely productive, particularly as the ivory, which is found in great abundance here, is of the first quality.

From Curimba Bar, the coast runs S.W. 6 leagues to Cape Angola, (or Palmarinho Point of the Portuguese) which is a low sandy point covered with palm trees, and a spit stretching from it a league into the sea.   It lies in 9° 14′ South latitude, and 13° 15′ East longitude, with Sleeper's Bay on the South side, and the River Coanza S. by E. 5½ leagues, which constitutes the southern extremity of the Angola Coast.

A Description of the Cape of Good Hope with its adjacent Bays.

The Cape of Good Hope is the Southern extremity of a mountanious peninsula, which terminates the great Continent of Africa, and which ships must round on their voyage from Europe to India, it was first discovered by the Portuguese in 1489, and from the violent winds and storms they encountered there, was, until late years, considered an object of extreme difficulty and danger to proceed by this passage, but which is now completely done away with, by our attainment of perfection in the art of navigation, as well as an accurate knowledge of the prevailing currents, and the seasons most proper for arriving in these latitudes.

The climate of the Cape is reckoned extremely salubrious. The spring commences in October continuing until December, and succeeded by the summer months, which last till March, during which period dry S.E. winds prevail, with frequent refreshing sea breezes from an early hour of the morning until noon. The autumn is from the fall of March to the end of May, and is almost as mild and agreeable as the spring, with the exception of rain, which it is more subject to. The winter months are June, July, and August, bringing with them cold, foggy, cloudy weather, and frequent boisterous N.W. winds, with violent rains. The approach of winter is announced by the S.E. wind blowing less frequently, or violently, also by the appearance of a white fleecy cloud on the Table Mountain ceasing to accompany it, as the approach of summer is announced by the increase of the one, and the appearance of the other.

The Pitch of the Cape lies in 34° 27' South latitude, and 18° 30' East longitude, with 2½ points westerly variation; at a short distance it bears the appearance of an island, all about which the land is remarkably lofty, of which Table Mountain is the highest and most striking, being the centre of a long range in the form of a crescent; it derives its name from the level surface of its summit, its height is about 4,000 feet above the level of the sea, bounded on each side by two great hills, the one to the East called the Lion's Head, or Devil's Mount, and the other to the West, the Tiger Hill, or Sugar Loaf.   P 2

The Peninsula is bordered by two commodious bays, the one on the N.W. shore, called Table Bay, the other on the S.E. called False Bay. The former receives its appellation from the name of the mountain, and is a large commodious but open roadsted, with Cape Town in front of the South end of the bay, being in 33° 58' S. latitude, and 18° 26' E. longitude. The current invariably runs strong to the Northward, which renders it necessary in sailing for the bay to make the land to the Southward. When off the Cape of Good Hope you may stand close along shore without danger, as far as Freeman's Point, where there is a ledge of rocks stretching seaward about a mile. Between this point and Sugar Loaf Hill is a bay of the same name. Abreast of Freeman's Point the ground is sandy, with from 50 to 53 fathoms, from thence steer for a low green point (called Green Point) before arriving whence the small Island of Penguim appears; to the right of which 1½ mile to the S.W. stretches a ledge and rock called the Whale, which only break in bad weather.

From the foot of the Sugar Loaf to Green Point there are several rocks above water, which give a good birth to as you run in, when you will shoal your water gradually from 30 to 10 fathoms to Green Point, which you may close in with to 8 fathoms without danger; then steer up the bay in from 8 to 6 fathoms, regular soundings but rocky until half a league to the Eastward of Green Point, where it is sandy and fit for anchorage.

You may anchor in Table Bay in 5 to 7 fathoms, within 1 mile abreast the town, good holding ground. There is anchorage also on the East side of Penguim Island, in 11 and 12 fathoms, 1½ mile off shore.

This bay is a safe and secure harbour from September until the middle of May, the wind being generaly off the land, though sometimes very boisterous; but after that period, when the violent N.W. winds commence, ships ought on no account to remain here; but proceed round to False Bay, which is so called from the promontory of land stretching into the sea, called Cape False. This bay is not properly the harbour, on this side the Peninsula, but the outer road of another smaller one, called Simon's Bay, in which vessels lie with great security, during the N.W. winds of the winter months; during the other months when the S.E. winds prevail, Simon's Bay is equally dangerous, which obliges ships to run into Table Bay. Simon's Bay is of an indented shape, almost surrounded by exceedingly high hills, with two remarkable rocks at the entrance, called the Roman Rocks, and Noah's ark, on which is a flag-staff; on the outer part of False Bay are some dangerous sunken rocks, on which, however, a buoy is placed to prevent accidents. It is high water on full and change days, at $2^H 30^I$ p. m. in the vicinity of the Cape.

The Island of St. Helena

Is nearly 400 leagues distant from the Coast of Africa. Its greatest length from Saddle Point to S.W. Point is 10 miles, and 7 in breadth, from James Town to Powell's Valley. Its approach presents the appearance of an accumulated heap of dreary rocks and mountains, the principal and highest of which is Diana's Peak, being 2700 feet above the level of the sea ; its shore is bold all round, but generally speaking inaccessible, from an uninterrupted chain of rocks, which renders it naturally strong and fortified. The principal landing places are at Rupert's Bay, James Town, and Lennon Valley on the leeward coast, and Sandy Bay to windward, all of which are well defended ; there are several ravines or vallies where it is possible for boats to land, if not opposed, but being excessively narrow and rugged, a very few men would effectually oppose the landing of the most numerous body.

The island of St. Helena was first discovered by the Portuguese, in the year 1502, on St. Helen's day, from whence it derives its name.

The climate is perhaps the mildest and most salubrious in the world, possessing a congenial medium temperature, which, however, varies considerably according to the elevation of the land. During the year there are two seasons of rains, the summer rains being in January and March, and those of winter, June and July. The winds throughout the year, are the trades from the S.E. with rare occurrences of westerly breezes, which sometimes continue five or six days.

JAMES TOWN, or the Seat of Government, is in 15° 55′ South latitude, and 5° 43′ West longitude, situated in the most leeward part of the island, at the entrance of James's Valley, so that ships sailing hence cannot with any certainty reach the town, without coming round the N.E. end, therefore run down the East side of the island, doubling Sugar Loaf Point, within a cable's length, which is bold without danger, here the trades generally cease, succeeded by, sometimes, powerful eddies, which if you do not hug the shore well aboard, you are liable to be blown off the bank.   On the West of the Point stands a small fort, about a mile S.W. from whence is Rupert's Valley, when you will find from 18 to 20 fathoms, next Munden's Point, and then James Town and Valley, off which is the place of anchorage.   The bank extends nearly 1½ mile N.W. of the fort, from 7 to 60 fathoms :   The best birth however is about 1¼ mile off shore, in from 8 to 15 fathoms, the Fort Flag-Staff bearing from S.E. to S. by E. coarse sand and gravel.   The best watering places are near James's Fort and at Lennon Valley.

Off Castle Rock Point to the Southward there are several rocks, called the Needles, which are obvious enough to be avoided.

From the circumstance of this island being small and liable to be missed, it is advisable to get into its latitude at some distance off, and run down its parallel, particularly as the current is strong in the trades, and would render it difficult to fetch it again in the event of running past.

The Island of Ascension.

This island was first discovered by the Portuguese in 1501, it is of volcanic origin, formed of almost barren mountains, surrounded by rugged rocks of lava, the broken pieces of which appear as if accumulated by art ; they rise to the height of about 40 feet from the shore, beyond whence is a level plain 6 or 8 miles in circuit, the earth in some parts is black, in others of a minute red dusty nature. Near the centre of the island rises a broad white mountain of gritty

tophaceous limestone, covered in many parts with patches of peculiar green grass,* from whence it is called the Green Mountain, it
is nearly 2400 feet above the level of the sea, and may be descried
at the distance of 12 leagues.

The anchorage is on the N.W. side of the island in a small inlet,
called Sandy Bay, which may be known by a ruddy cone-formed
hill, on which there is a cross, hence its appellation, Cross Hill ;
for anchoring, bring this hill to bear about S.S.E. half a mile off
shore, in 9 or 10 fathoms, sand and gravel, where it is good holding ground and perfectly safe, as the wind invariably blows off
shore.

The Western extremity of the bay, called Rocky Point, must
be avoided, on account of a reef stretching from it a mile to seaward, which breaks in bad weather. The bay lies in 7° 35′ South
latitude, and 14° 16′ West longitude. The seasons and climate
are nearly similar to those of St. Helena.

The island abounds in purslane, turtle, goats, and fish, but badly
supplied with fresh water.

Vessels bound to Ascension, are advised to sail along the North
side of it, within two cables' lengths of the shore, which is bold
and steep, until Cross Hill is brought into the centre of Sandy Bay,
the place of anchorage.

Since the residence of Buonaparte at St. Helena, the English
have established a Fort and Signal Post at this island, under the
command of a lieutenant of the navy, it is consequently more frequented than usual, particularly by men of war from the African
station, in running from whence to make it, observe the aforesaid
directions, for first gaining the trades, and then shape a course for
the island.

---

*Aristida Adscensionis.

Of the Passages to and from the Coast of Africa, &c.

In the directions for navigating from the English Channel to the Coast of Africa, and across the equator towards the Cape of Good Hope and the East Indies; various ideas have been suggested, and many tracks laid down for the better guidance of vessels; but the experience and scientific knowledge of modern navigators, have from principles of practice and well regulated theory, reduced the navigation of those passages to one undeviating system, which if strictly adhered to, must in a general point of view ensure the shortest possible passage.

A few preliminary observations will be necessary, respecting the winds and currents peculiar to the frequented tracks; for instance, the perennial or trade winds caused as before observed, by the earth's rotatory motion, and rarefaction of the atmosphere, are known to blow through the year without intermission, from the N.E. and S.E. which are found however to vary in their limits; the former or N.E. commence upon an average between the latitudes of 4° and 8° North, and terminate in from 28° and sometimes 38° North, being more Easterly, if the sun has high North declination, but farther North with South declination.   The limits of the S.E. trades, are between 3 or 4 degrees North to the equator, extending to 18 and 26 South, and are Easterly when the sun has great South declination, and the contrary with North declination. The intervening space between these winds is generally attended with calms and squalls, or breezes from the South and S.W. which latter are most prevalent; this space is greater to the Eastward, diminishing as you approach the confluence of the two winds to the Westward, where it frequently gradually changes round from S.E. to N.E. without any material interval.

There are also spaces of calm between the trade winds, and the variables in high latitudes, caused by the conflux of each other from opposite points, and are oftentimes excessively tedious; a long series of such weather, may be generally observed to precede a storm, and most frequently occurs when the trades are farthest from the East.

The currents of the Atlantic are from well ascertained facts, known to proceed from the action of the wind; consequently the stream which prevails in the equatorial regions from East to West, may be correctly assigned to the permanency of the trade winds, which produce an equal uniformity of current, that is more or less rapid, according to the velocity of the breeze, and has Northing or Southing in proportion as the trades incline towards the tropics. However, for vessels sailing West of all the African islands, bound across the line, or along the S.E. and across the N.E. trades homeward, 1¼ mile per hour to the Westward is found, from experience, to be the allowance requisite to produce the nearest attainable accuracy without the aid of chronometers or lunar observations.

There is also a strong Northerly current found to prevail between the two trades for which half a mile per hour must be allowed, during the period of traversing that space.

If bound to the East-Indies, shape a course from the English Channel so as to pass Cape Finisterre at a distance of 60 leagues, and even more should the appearance of the weather indicate a probability of Westerly winds, and make Porto Santo, or the Island of Madeira, from whence you may take your departure; but if in possession of good chronometers, or the means of ascertaining the longitude by lunars, go to the Westward of all, on account of the winds being there fresher and more regular; and take care, by all means, to avoid the Coast of Africa, and not to approach nearer the Cape Verdes than at least 3 degrees, that you may avoid those calms and constant rains which, as before-described, exist in their vicinity.

When well to the Southward of these islands, steer to the S.E. so as to cross the equator not farther to the Westward than 20° that you may be able to clear the Coast of Brazil, in the event of the S.E. winds being far Southerly.

———

If bound to the Coast of Africa, a totally different route must be adopted ; for example : endeavour, as before, to gain a sight of Porto Santo, and shape a course from thence, so as to pass to the Westward of the Salvages, and between Palma and Teneriffe, which, from frequent observation, is found to be the most speedy and secure track for vessels on this voyage ; it is, however, by many considered essential to go to the Westward of these islands, but the time lost in making the necessary circuitous route to avoid the calms of the Canaries, is, from well digested experience, dis- covered to be infinitely greater than that in traversing the midst of them.

From Teneriffe regulate your course according to the point of destination. If bound to the Senegal, steer about S.S.W. to the latitude of 18° when you may haul to the Eastward for the port.

If to Goree, the Gambia, or Sierra Leon, endeavour to make Cape Verde, but if to the windward coast, keep amid-channel be- tween Cape Verde and the islands, hauling to the S.E. from the latitude of 10° or 12° North, so as to make the land about Cape St. Ann, or Cape Mount, the latter of which is the most preferable, being high land and recognizable at a considerable distance.

It is too frequently the very erroneous custom amongst the mas- ters of vessels employed in the African trade, to go outside the Cape Verde Islands, being without discrimination, guided by those di- rections which apply solely to ships bound across the line to the East Indies or elsewhere ; whereby they evidently expose them- selves to considerable detention : for in order to make the land about the windward coast, they must necessarily traverse those regions, which are so condemned to almost incessant rains and calms ; and which it is expressly intended and specified they should avoid.

On the Homeward Passage.

Much depends on the part of the coast, from whence vessels are sailing for the track on which they are to proceed home; for instance, from Senegal, Goree, or Sierra Leon, you may stand off to gain the N.E. trades immediately, and thereby make a rapid passage; from Cape Coast, and the ports within the bights of Benin and Biaffra, it is necessary to cross the line, in order to gain the S.E. trades, to carry you to the Westward, clear of the African coast and islands. On crossing the equator therefore, go as far as 3° South, where you will find fresh trades, (commencing the before-mentioned allowance for current on reaching them) and sail along that parallel as far as 28 or 30° West, where you may re-cross the line.

In this vicinity take care of the island of St. Paul's, which lies in 29° 35′ West, and according to different authorities, in 54 miles North, which latitude is widely erroneous, for it is considerably farther to the Northward, but owing to thick weather, the author was unable to ascertain the accuracy of its position, which therefore still remains a desideratum. The island is composed of a cluster of barren spiral rocks, with a pond of excellent fresh water on the summit of the main one, and a bold shore all round. Portuguese vessels have oftentimes been known to water here in cases of distress, by parbuckling their casks up and down the rock.

To the inexperienced, 30° appear an unreasonable and unnecessary distance, to run out of the direct course, but concurring evidence and self-experience of the author, have proved, the farther we proceed West, the less we feel those intervals of variable weather; and on the contrary, obtain steadier and stronger winds, which gradually draw round from the S.E. to the N.E.

The generality of African traders are in the habit of crossing in 18° or 20° and from thence (if the N.E. winds are far Easterly) make the Cape Verdes, which is wilfully running into those obstacles and difficulties they are directed to avoid, by going to the South and Westward, and to which may be attributed, the tedious voyages that are frequently made in that trade, to the great detriment of the merchant: Let it be therefore observed, on crossing in the

above specified longitude, not to come again to the Eastward, how-ever favourable the wind may prove, but to pass to the Westward of the Azores, and by no means to the Eastward, on account of the adverse winds that so frequently prevail between them and the coast of Portugal.

Should the N.E trades be far Northerly, do not hug the wind too closely, but keep your sails well filled in crossing them, without being alarmed if you are thrown off to the Westward, even as far as from 40° to 46°, but continue on the same tack, and you will find the wind will gradually and successively draw round to the S.W. West and N.W. ultimately ensuring you a rapid passage to the Eastward. According to the foregoing track, and observations the author has made the passage from the Bight of Biaffra, to the river Mersey in seven weeks, which, other vessels are, generally speaking, ten, twelve, and thirteen weeks in performing, by crossing the line farther to the Eastward, and proceeding in a more direct course to the Northward.

A TABLE

THE LATITUDES AND LONGITUDES

OF

THE MOST PRINCIPAL PLACES ON THE WEST COAST.

	Latitude.			Longitude.		
	o	'	''	o	l.	''
Cape Blanco ·································						
Cape Verde ······· ·······················	14	48	0	17	36	0 W.
Goree Island ·····························						
Cape St. Mary ···· ·······················	13	6	0	16	40	0
The West End of Tamara, of the Isles de Loss	9	25	0 N.	13	27	0 W.
Cape Sierra Leon ·······················...	8	30	0	13	10	0
The North End of St. Ann's Shoals ··········	8	10	0 N.	13	36	0 W.
Cape St. Ann ·····························	7	8	0	12	36	0
Cape Mount ·······························	6	44	0	11	34	0
Cape Mounserrado ·························	6	14	0	11	26	0
River Sesters ·····························	3	34	0 N.	9	46	0 W.
Cape Palmas ·········· ·············· ···	4	25	0	8	13	0
Cape Lahou ·······························	5	17	0 N.	5	20	0 W.
Cape Appolonia ························ ·.....	5	0	0 N.	3	24	0 W.
Cape Three Points ················ · ······	4	41	0			
Cape Coast ·······················-········	5	2	0	2	3	0
Cape St. Paul's································	5	50	0	0	57	0 East
Lagos····································· · ··	6	13	0	3	1	0 East
The N. W. Head of Benin River ·············	5	34	0	4	55	0
Cape Formoso ····················· ·········	4	20	0	5	55	0 East
Tom Shot's Point·····························	4	24	0 N.	8	55	0 East
Fernandepo, the North End ·················	3	40	0 N.	8	40	0 East
Princes Island ········· ·················	1	38	0 N.	7	10	0 East
St. Thomas ⎰ ·························	0	30	0 N.	6	37	0 East
Anna de Chaves ⎱						
Anno Bom ······························	1	30	0 S.	5	30	0
Cape Cameroons ·····················...······	3	37	0 N.	9	20	0 East
Cape St. John ····························	1	16	0 N.	8	40	0 East
Cape Clara ·······························	0	25	0 N.	8	35	0 East
Cape Lopez ······················· ·····...	1	9	0 S.			
Cape St. Catherine ·······················				9	35	0 East
Cape Mayumba ·························	3	35	0 S.	11	15	0 East
Indian Bar ⎰ ·························	4	37	0 S.	12	30	0 East
Loango Bay ⎱						
Point Palmar········· ·················						
Cape Padron ·····························	6	15	0 S.	12	34	0 East
Ambriz Bay ·····························	8	2	0 S.	13	10	0 East
Dandè Point··············· ················.						
Cape Angola ⎰ ·························	9	14	0	13	15	0
Sleeper's Bay ⎱						
Cape of Good Hope ·························	34	27	0 S.	18	30	0 East
Island of St. Helena, James's Town ··········	15	55	0 S.	5	43	0 W.
Island of Ascension, Sandy Bay ·····.·······	7	35	0 S.	14	16	0 W.

FINIS.

Printed by H. Gye, Market-Place, Bath.

For EU product safety concerns, contact us at Calle de José Abascal, 56–1°, 28003 Madrid, Spain or eugpsr@cambridge.org.

www.ingramcontent.com/pod-product-compliance
Ingram Content Group UK Ltd.
Pitfield, Milton Keynes, MK11 3LW, UK
UKHW012338130625
459647UK00009B/378